National Disaster Recovery Framework – Third Edition

This page left intentionally blank.

National Disaster Recovery Framework – Third Edition

Contents

1. Introduction 1
    1.1. Purpose 1
    1.2. Audience 1
    1.3. Scope 1
    1.4. National Preparedness Goal 2
2. Disaster Recovery Overview 2
    2.1. Introduction to Disaster Recovery 2
    2.2. Disaster Recovery Begins During Response 3
    2.3 Achieving Successful Disaster Recovery Outcomes 4
3. Federal Roles and Responsibilities 6
    3.1. FEMA Leadership in the Field 6
    3.2. Interagency Recovery Coordination 7
    3.3. Federal Recovery Support Functions 7
4. State, Local, Tribal Nation, and Territorial Roles and Responsibilities 18
    4.1. Local Governments 20
    4.2. States and Territories 20
    4.3. Tribal Nations 21
5. Nongovernmental Resources 22
    5.1. Long-Term Recovery Groups 22
    5.2. Nongovernmental Organizations 23
    5.3. Philanthropy, Business and Industry, and Academia 24
6. Conclusion 26

Appendix A: Recovery Support Functions and Participating Agencies and Organizations A-1
Appendix B: Acronyms B-1
Appendix C: Glossary C-1
Appendix D: Pre-disaster Recovery Planning and Post-disaster Recovery Planning D-1
Appendix E: Digital Resource Links E-1
Appendix F: National Preparedness Goal Core Capabilities F-1
Appendix G: Document Updates and Maintenance G-1

Figures

Figure 1: Disaster Recovery Lifecycle 2
Figure 2: Recovery Continuum 3
Figure 3: Community-Driven Recovery 18

Tables

Table 1: Acronyms B-1

Table 2: Pre-disaster Recovery Planning D-1

Table 3: Post-disaster Recovery Planning D-2

Table 4: Strategies for Measuring Progress Through Data D-3

Table 5: NPG Recovery Core Capabilities F-1

1. Introduction

1.1. Purpose

Communities nationwide face many threats and hazards, including biological, climate-related,[1] human-caused, natural, and technological. The guiding principle of the National Disaster Recovery Framework (NDRF) is that disaster recovery is most successful when it is organized around community-driven and locally defined goals that promote fairness and support resilient outcomes. This guiding principle applies to both pre-and post-disaster activities and recognizes that intentional intergovernmental and cross-sector collaboration is crucial for developing recovery strategies and projects that help achieve the disaster recovery goals of state, local, Tribal Nation,[2] and territorial governments (SLTTs).

The NDRF outlines the federal government's approach for providing disaster recovery resources and support. It also explains the federal government's roles and responsibilities for organizing and deploying disaster recovery assistance. The NDRF enhances effective collaboration among federal agencies and SLTTs and informs nongovernmental partners.

As a national framework, the NDRF describes high-level disaster recovery roles and responsibilities. SLTTs may use the federal structure as a model to guide and inform their own disaster recovery planning and policymaking. The NDRF model can be applied across a broad range of disasters, not just those that receive a federal disaster declaration.

1.2. Audience

The NDRF is primarily written for SLTT officials, who are the main counterparts to federal recovery officials. By understanding the federal recovery structure, SLTT officials responsible for guiding their community's recovery can more effectively lead and coordinate disaster recovery efforts. This framework is also valuable for recovery practitioners at all levels, whether they serve in a formal or informal recovery role during disasters. Disaster recovery practitioners include full time professionals, like state and county emergency managers, as well as individuals from across the whole community.

1.3. Scope

The NDRF explains how the federal government supports disaster-affected SLTTs as they recover and describes federal and nongovernmental recovery resources that may be available to SLTTs under federal declarations. This includes support under:

- Stafford Act declarations (e.g., emergency and major disaster declarations);
- Agency declarations (e.g., public health emergencies, drought disasters); and
- Presidentially directed disaster recovery support (e.g., through Executive Order or a Presidential Memorandum).

While the NDRF describes how the federal government mobilizes for disaster recovery, it recognizes that communities constantly respond to and recover from disasters that do not receive federal declarations. The concepts presented within the NDRF can be adapted by communities so they can be better equipped to recover and rebuild in a resilient and sustainable manner.

---

[1] US Global Change Research Program, Fifth National Climate Assessment, 2023.
[2] Usage of Tribal Nations herein refers to the list of federally recognized Tribal Nations maintained by Department of the Interior pursuant to the Federally Recognized Indian Tribe List Act of 1994.

1.4. National Preparedness Goal

The National Preparedness Goal (NPG) outlines five mission areas: prevention, protection, mitigation, response, and recovery. It also describes the corresponding core capabilities (see Appendix F: National Preparedness Goal Core Capabilities for more information) necessary to achieve a secure and resilient nation. By incorporating principles of resilience the NDRF enhances the coordination of disaster recovery efforts and strengthens whole community resilience. The National Resilience Guidance emphasizes that resilience requires a collective approach and ongoing engagement with whole community partners. Similarly, the NDRF underscores the importance of resilience throughout the disaster recovery process. This approach ensures effective recovery and contributes to broader preparedness for future disasters, to ultimately foster more robust and adaptable national resilience.

2. Disaster Recovery Overview

2.1. Introduction to Disaster Recovery

Disaster recovery is complex. Threats and hazards present emerging and intersecting risks to SLTTs, including increasingly severe and frequent weather events, hazardous materials incidents, and catastrophic technological disasters. Communities may still be recovering from one disaster when another occurs. Disaster recovery is not a linear or straightforward process but is cyclical and evolves based on the unique needs of each community. Mitigation, response, recovery, and rebuilding are highly interdependent and often occur simultaneously. Recovery efforts may be disrupted, delayed, or forced to restart as new disasters arise. New incidents may derail or set back a community's ongoing efforts, requiring them to pivot or revisit earlier recovery stages. This complexity highlights the need for flexible approaches that account for the interconnected nature of recovery operations.

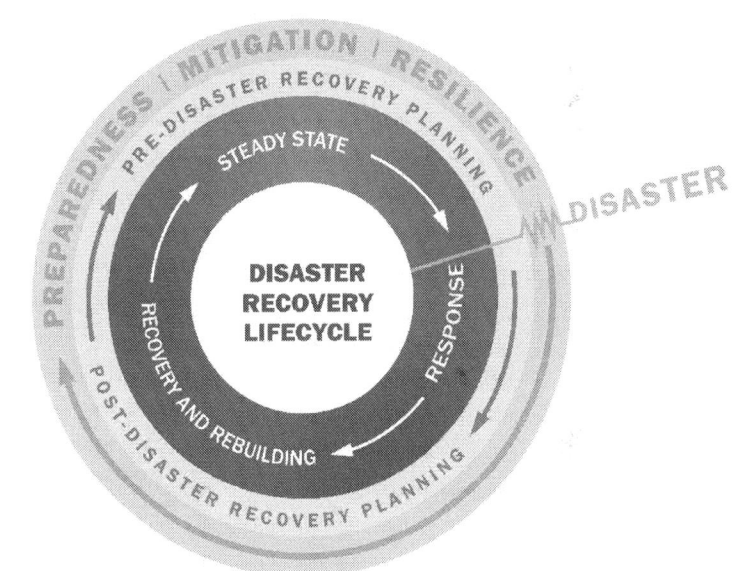

Figure 1: Disaster Recovery Lifecycle

Recovery is a cyclical, interdependent process where response, rebuilding, and mitigation often overlap. Progress may be disrupted or reset by new disasters, requiring flexible, adaptive approaches.

Adding to this complexity, demographics, geography, history, and countless other unique community factors require disaster recovery to be adaptable and accessible. Just as no two communities are the same, no two recoveries will look the same. Recovering from a disaster and rebuilding a community are very personal undertakings. Therefore, communities are best positioned to identify their own disaster recovery needs, priorities, goals, and objectives. Communities should take the lead in determining their disaster recovery milestones while also considering program-specific federal support deadlines.

National Disaster Recovery Framework – Third Edition

2.2. Disaster Recovery Begins During Response

During disaster response, the federal government seeks to address the needs of affected communities through lifesaving and life-sustaining operations and by stabilizing community lifelines,[3] which are the most fundamental services in a community that support the functioning of society. Officials coordinate initial response efforts as identified in the National Response Framework (NRF) and the Response and Recovery Federal Interagency Operational Plan (FIOP), and actions taken during the response phase often have a major impact on recovery efforts. This coordination is important to ensure continuity and alignment between response and recovery efforts – from stabilization to recovery planning and implementation.

The transition from response to recovery is marked by several indicators, such as the stabilization of immediate threats to life and property, and the restoration of essential community lifelines. As these indicators emerge, federal engagement in recovery begins, with officials shifting their focus to assessing and addressing recovery needs. Federal recovery officials coordinate with their response counterparts and may be co-located at coordination centers to share information. They use data collected during the response phase to understand the extent of damage and disruption to impacted communities. This information guides early recovery activities such as conducting preliminary damage assessments and identifying unmet needs. Critical information on damaged infrastructure, affected populations, and overall needs of the community provide a foundation for early recovery actions.

It is imperative to consider and incorporate recovery priorities and outcomes during early post-disaster goal setting. Recovery goals can be both near-term (e.g., restoration of disaster affected publicly owned infrastructure, reopening schools, supporting temporary housing solutions, implementing debris removal plans) and long-term (e.g., housing implementation plans, economic recovery). Information obtained during response such as geospatial damage assessments, among other data sets, can serve as the foundation for developing a Recovery Needs Assessment and disaster recovery plans. As community lifelines are stabilized, the decision to transition from response to recovery and rebuilding sets the stage for sustainable and resilient outcomes.

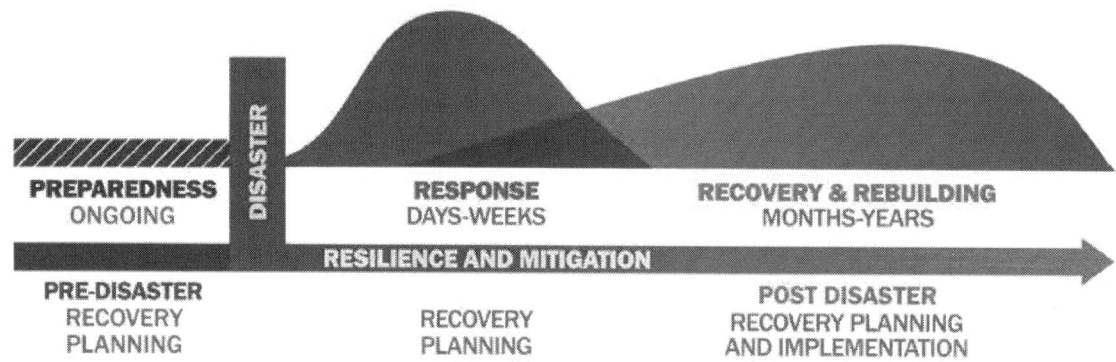

Figure 2: Recovery Continuum

The Recovery Continuum depicts how recovery efforts begin alongside response activities, and gradually scale up during response operations, highlighting the relationship across these phases. Enhancing resilience through mitigation and other risk management strategies spans the entire continuum, guiding the recovery and rebuilding process. Investments in mitigation and resilience will enable a community's ability to prepare for threats and hazards, adapt to changing conditions, and withstand and recover rapidly from adverse conditions and disruptions.

---

[3] There are eight community lifelines: Safety and Security; Food, Hydration and Shelter; Health and Medical; Energy; Communications; Transportation; Hazardous Materials; and Water Systems. Federal Emergency Management Agency (FEMA), Community Lifelines, 2024.

2.3 Achieving Successful Disaster Recovery Outcomes

A community-driven, locally executed strategy is critical to successful disaster recovery. Every community has unique recovery priorities based on its circumstances, challenges, and resources. For example, some communities may conclude that success requires relocating part or all of their infrastructure to mitigate future risks. Others may pursue more resilient building practices, thereby decreasing vulnerability to weather and climate hazards. Ultimately, successful disaster recovery plans are shaped by the community, clearly communicated, and pursued as part of a unified effort across all disaster recovery partners.

The disaster recovery process seeks to help communities achieve their disaster recovery goals. A clear understanding of how all disaster recovery practitioners can best work together maximizes a community's ability to leverage available resources. This collaboration supports goals such as resilience, sustainability, and measuring progress with data. These topics are further discussed in subsequent sections.

DISASTER RECOVERY PLANNING AND RESILIENCE[4]

Disaster recovery planning presents a unique opportunity to mitigate future risks by rebuilding in a resilient and sustainable manner.[5] Effective recovery planning, whether conducted pre- or post-disaster, is important to enhance community resilience. Active and continuous disaster recovery planning allows SLTTs to assess their current situation, set recovery goals, and develop strategies to achieve them.

Pre-disaster recovery planning enables SLTTs to set priorities, establish goals, assess capabilities, identify gaps, and determine the resources needed before a disaster. This proactive approach strengthens partner communication, supports measuring recovery progress, and fosters resilience. By identifying existing threats, hazards, risks, vulnerabilities, and resources, communities can enhance resilience and develop mitigation strategies including adaptation strategies for extreme weather events. Incorporating meaningful mitigation opportunities throughout the disaster recovery process maximizes future resilience and minimizes risks. Communities should leverage existing mitigation plans when possible, and rigorously assess community factors that may hinder disaster recovery or long-term resilience and sustainability goals.

Planning should also address whole community fairness and cultural considerations to ensure disaster recovery efforts are inclusive and community-driven. Disaster recovery plans should engage diverse residents, leaders, and organizations from across the whole community. To prioritize outreach and ensure fair representation, it is essential to include all cultures, populations, and groups, including historically marginalized communities, varying socio-economic statuses, and people with disabilities and other access and functional needs. Where applicable, recovery plans should also be inclusive of natural and cultural resources, sacred sites, traditional homelands, and areas used for subsistence hunting and fishing. By committing to accessible physical spaces, programs, and communication, recovery planning can better meet the emerging needs of the whole community. This approach supports successful post-disaster recovery and strengthens community resilience by developing social trust.

Disaster recovery plans should be easy to access and align with existing planning resources to ensure coordination across sectors and governments. To the extent feasible, post-disaster recovery planning should also align with the community's existing planning processes involving relevant federal and non-federal departments and entities as appropriate.

---

[4] Resilience is defined in the National Resilience Guidance as the ability to prepare for threats and hazards, adapt to changing conditions, and withstand and recover rapidly from adverse conditions and disruptions.
[5] Mitigating future risks includes addressing shocks and stressors, considering the dependencies and interdependencies between systems. See National Resilience Guidance for more information on shocks and stressors.

Resilience planners, including resilience officials, hazard mitigation planners, and community resilience champions can help strengthen community systems, much like recovery planners. During rebuilding, communities can pursue opportunities that achieve multiple objectives to support resilience, sustainability, and livability. Examples include fostering growth, making smart energy choices, improving economic competitiveness, expanding accessible housing options, and enhancing healthy, safe, walkable neighborhoods in all community areas.

For detailed examples of pre- and post-disaster recovery planning activities, see Appendix D. Further information is provided in Appendix E: Digital Resource Links, including recovery planning and resilience resources such as Pre-Disaster Recovery Planning Guides for SLTTs and the Pre-Disaster Housing Planning Guide.

> **Helping Small Businesses Navigate Recovery Planning**
>
> The Small Business Administration's (SBA) Business Resilience Guide is a comprehensive resource for small business owners who may not be familiar with disaster preparation. This easy-to-follow guide leads business owners through creating a robust resilience plan and has six sections on how to plan for and recover from disasters. It includes best practices and template forms that guide America's entrepreneurs in their business recovery planning and rebuilding. SBA also provides practical tools to support small businesses with its online learning content, available at www.sba.gov. The website hosts educational content that is free to small business owners and entrepreneurs including a learning journey entitled "Disaster and Economic Recovery." This journey has been the most used educational content on SBA's online learning platform since its launch in 2021 and covers the impacts of disasters and disaster recovery strategies including how to access financial assistance following a disaster.

LEVERAGING DATA

Data and analytical tools are useful for conducting damage assessments, informing pre- and post-disaster recovery planning, and tracking progress toward disaster recovery goals. These tools support data-driven decision making by providing a common understanding of recovery objectives, guiding resource allocation, and identifying impacts.

To maximize the benefits of data-driven decision making, SLTTs should consider data integrity, fair representation in data collection, and the careful selection of data sets and tools, while also identifying and addressing data gaps. SLTTs may also consider methods to ensure data sources are integrated, comprehensive, accurate, and reliable (e.g., establishing and maintaining data sharing agreements with relevant agencies and partners). Local public records can provide insights into useful services to forecast needs or complete assessments.

Some communities may choose to request technical assistance or guidance to enhance their use of data in pre- and post-disaster recovery plans, and to analyze information collected prior to or during response efforts. This support may be sought from federal agencies, data experts, or consultants. Many recovery partners develop analytical tools to assist SLTT decision making, progress tracking, and resource allocation (see Appendix A for some examples of analytical tools).

MEASURING PROGRESS THROUGHOUT RECOVERY

Measuring and communicating progress throughout disaster recovery can increase public confidence by promoting transparency, accountability, and shared outcomes. Key indicators and recovery measures can vary by community based on disaster impacts and available data. Establishing these recovery goals early allows local leaders and partners at all levels to collaborate effectively, align strategies, and identify gaps, resources, and needed support. This process also helps communities develop lessons learned for future planning and continuous improvement priorities.

Communities can develop metrics and gather data that track progress on disaster recovery outcomes. While some metrics may be common across disaster recovery missions, each community is likely to have its own methods for measuring success. Common recovery metrics include the percentage of homes rebuilt, diversification of economic portfolios, the amount of disaster recovery funding applied for and spent, and the number of completed projects. Additionally, metrics might track services provided by voluntary organizations and progress in specific time periods (e.g., monthly, quarterly, annually). Community-specific improvements, such as establishing a farmers' market in a food desert or forming a partnership to establish a grocery store, can also be measured to address pre-existing disparities and enhance access to essential resources within a community.

3. Federal Roles and Responsibilities

The federal government can play a critical role in helping disaster-affected SLTTs recover and rebuild. Individual federal agencies can provide recovery support through multiple avenues, including their statutory authorities, ongoing steady state programs, established partnerships, and regional offices. This includes Federal Emergency Management Agency (FEMA) field leadership roles, which are activated following Stafford Act declarations, as well as the six federal interagency Recovery Support Functions (RSFs). Once immediate response priorities are addressed, recovery activities begin with federal and SLTT agencies collaborating to assess needs and coordinate recovery efforts.

3.1. FEMA Leadership in the Field

When FEMA supports disaster recovery, it designates key individuals to represent the agency in the impacted area. Three critical field roles carry significant responsibilities: the Federal Coordinating Officer (FCO) and Federal Disaster Recovery Coordinator (FDRC), who serve as primary field leaders upon deployment, and the Federal Disaster Recovery Officer (FDRO), who leads the coordination among federal interagency partners and collaborates closely with the FCOs and FDRCs. These leaders work together with federal headquarters and regional offices to engage SLTT officials and recovery representatives, initiating discussions on recovery goals, objectives, and outcomes early in the disaster recovery process. The FCO, FDRC, and FDRO ensure communication and outreach engages all partners by working closely with SLTT counterparts to support the recovery mission.

FEDERAL COORDINATING OFFICER

For emergency and major disaster declarations under the Stafford Act, the president appoints an FCO to implement an operational coordination structure in close collaboration with SLTT response and recovery leadership. The FCO serves as the counterpart to the lead state, territory, or Tribal Nation response official and has primary responsibility for coordinating federal disaster response and recovery support to the whole community in accordance with the NRF, NDRF, and Federal Interagency Operational Plans (FIOPs). The FCO leads the Joint Field Office (JFO), the central post-disaster coordinating point for federal resources located within or near the affected community.

FEDERAL DISASTER RECOVERY COORDINATOR

In complex missions, the FDRC may be assigned to lead recovery integration efforts across the federal interagency and SLTTs through Interagency Recovery Coordination (IRC) and FEMA programs. The FDRC is the federal counterpart to the lead state, territory, and Tribal Nation recovery officials and integrates the IRC team into the JFO. The FDRC serves as the primary conduit for recovery information, helping affected communities establish recovery goals while addressing interagency opportunities, challenges, and gaps at the senior level.

The FDRC integrates FEMA recovery programs and RSF operations and activities, while engaging with SLTT counterparts, business and industry, voluntary, faith-based, disability advocacy, philanthropic, and community organizations. This role facilitates the development of a recovery plan that aligns with local recovery goals. The FDRC also facilitates the alignment of federal resources to help communities implement their recovery plans and achieve their recovery goals.

FEDERAL DISASTER RECOVERY OFFICER

The FDRO, under the leadership of the FCO or FDRC, leads the IRC mission and is the primary contact for federal interagency recovery partners. The FDRO engages affected SLTTs to understand their recovery priorities and coordinate delivery of federal recovery support. Responsibilities include IRC staffing based on the size and scope of projected interagency engagements and managing the strategic direction of field activities identified by the RSF Field Coordinators to ensure unity of effort among federal agencies.

The FDRO aligns the work of the RSF Field Coordinators, who receive their strategic direction from the RSF National Coordinators. The FDRO coordinates RSF mission priorities, enhances situational awareness and reporting across recovery operations, organizes daily disaster recovery activities, facilitates the development of a Recovery Needs Assessment, and supports the development and implementation of a comprehensive recovery strategy. Additionally, the FDRO advises the FCO and FDRC on key recovery issues and projects.

3.2. Interagency Recovery Coordination

The mission of Interagency Recovery Coordination (IRC) is to help SLTTs achieve their recovery outcomes effectively, efficiently, and fairly. When activated by the FCO after a major disaster declaration, IRC mobilizes federal agencies and non-federal partners to collectively identify community recovery needs, set priorities, and implement solutions to achieve recovery outcomes. By using an outcome-driven strategic approach, IRC missions provide tangible assistance to SLTTs and impacted communities throughout disaster recovery. It also enhances communication and coordination among FEMA, federal agencies, SLTTs, and other members of the IRC mission to streamline recovery efforts.

The goal of the IRC mission is to convene federal interagency and non-federal resources to help SLTTs navigate the complex recovery landscape, including identifying unmet needs, gaps, and recovery priorities. Additionally, the IRC guides communities through the range of available support from federal agencies, academia, nonprofit organizations, nongovernmental organizations (NGOs), voluntary organizations, and business and industry partners.

> **Interagency Collaboration: Vermont Recovery Structure**
>
> In early July 2023, severe storms in Vermont caused significant flooding, landslides, and mudslides. The disaster created many challenges for individuals, households, and public and private infrastructure. After President Biden declared a major disaster for Vermont, FEMA Region 1 collaborated with the state to identify and address the state's recovery priorities. Vermont organized eight Recovery Task Forces, as counterparts to the six federal RSFs. The IRC mission played an important role in aligning these task forces with the appropriate federal RSFs. This alignment ensured efficient, coordinated support and demonstrated the IRC's purpose: to facilitate collaboration among state and federal agencies, enabling a flexible and adaptive response to evolving recovery needs. By fostering this collaboration, the IRC worked to effectively address Vermont's complex recovery challenges.

3.3. Federal Recovery Support Functions

INTRODUCTION TO RECOVERY SUPPORT FUNCTIONS

Disaster recovery often requires expertise outside of emergency management to solve problems. In Stafford Act declarations, as well as for other federally supported disaster recoveries, the federal government may activate RSFs as part of the IRC to serve as the coordinating structure to organize and streamline federal disaster recovery assistance.

The RSFs are six capabilities of federal interagency support and expertise:

> Community Assistance | Economic | Health, Education, and Human Services |
> Housing | Infrastructure Systems | Natural and Cultural Resources |

RSFs are led by a federal Coordinating Agency designated based on the agency's expertise and resources, and comprised of federal agencies and organizations with relevant capabilities and expertise. In addition, other departments, agencies, and organizations may participate in a federal RSF's mission as needed. These agencies work together within and across RSFs to address the needs of the community and ensure a comprehensive approach to disaster recovery.

Each RSF has a unique mission aligned with its focus area, aimed at achieving strategic outcomes through collaboration with SLTTs and nongovernmental partners. RSFs are designed to improve solution-oriented coordination among recovery officials, practitioners, relevant partners, and experts. By leveraging collective expertise, resources, and capacity, RSFs strengthen communication and coordination in preparation for future incidents. While RSF activations are based on the needs of the community, federal partners may alternate leadership roles throughout the recovery process depending on which agency's expertise is most needed. There are no pre-determined timelines for when RSF support ends; timing is determined by the evolving needs of the affected community.

SLTTs may also use the federal structure to develop, adopt, or adapt their own RSF structures and coordinate pre- and post-disaster recovery planning and operations. The federal government is responsible for strategically aligning with the state, Tribal Nation, or territory and their preferred structure. More detailed RSF information, including examples of disaster assistance provided, is available in Appendix A.

RECOVERY SUPPORT FUNCTION ROLES AND RESPONSIBILITIES

Federal RSFs can provide in-person or virtual support based on the request of the SLTT and the capacity of the federal agencies activated. RSF staff and assets may deploy to support interagency coordination and cross-cutting projects identified by the community's recovery priorities. Federal RSF support can be requested individually or collectively to address the critical needs of the community, including direct agency Mission Assignments based on disaster recovery needs. Disaster recovery support may scale up later in the recovery continuum depending on what services RSFs provide and when the affected community is ready to receive that assistance.

Once activated, RSFs closely coordinate with SLTTs, partners, and community leaders to achieve recovery outcomes and support resilient recovery by helping a community reach its overall goals. RSF roles and responsibilities include:

- Coordinate with relevant SLTTs, nongovernmental partners, and other counterparts based on community needs.
- Develop a Recovery Needs Assessment to evaluate the disaster's impact on local and regional communities and systems by identifying key gaps, needs, and priorities.
- Develop a Recovery Support Strategy, based on the findings of the Recovery Needs Assessment and utilizing various sources outlining specific approaches and actions to address identified recovery needs and increase community resilience.
- Support SLTT partners to navigate available federal resources and advise on methods to optimize resources, such as:

National Disaster Recovery Framework – Third Edition

- o **Financial Assistance** – Program-specific financial assistance, disaster loans, and grant opportunities to help SLTTs plan for and recover from disasters. The Recovery and Resilience Resource Library[6] can help navigate available federal support opportunities.
- o **Training** – Training opportunities that help communities build disaster recovery skillsets by learning through education and exercising recovery processes and policies. This supports SLTT capacity building, which fosters resilient communities and effective recovery (Appendix E: Digital Resource Links provides various training opportunities).
- o **Technical Assistance** – Support or services to SLTTs in implementing policies, processes, programs, metrics, operating systems, tools, and other similar projects. This aims to build SLTT capacity, address any existing challenges, and enhance federal-SLTT collaboration.
- o **Technical Expertise** – Specialized knowledge, skills, and experience from experts to help SLTTs use federal resources effectively. This can be accessed during a recovery through deployed FEMA assets in the field, FEMA regional offices, RSF Field Coordinators, and/or RSF Advisors.

Maui Wildfires: Creating A Strong Team

The 2023 Maui wildfires presented a major challenge and opportunity for interagency collaboration. Response and recovery operations immediately integrated many federal agencies, and FEMA coordinated across partners to provide technical assistance and expertise to the community. Agencies like the Department of Energy, U.S. Forest Service, and the Environmental Protection Agency – in addition to the federal RSF coordinating agencies – brought critical resources and expertise to address a variety of recovery challenges on Maui, including infrastructure repair and environmental remediation. For example, the IRC worked with the Council for Native Hawaiian Advancement to open the Kakoʻo Maui Resource Hub, to provide resources to kānaka maoli (Native Hawaiians) and kamaʻāina (Hawaiʻi residents from any racial, ethnic, or cultural group) in a culturally focused, comfortable space. Ultimately, this interagency collaboration helped produce Maui's long-term recovery plan which will serve the community in the years to come.

Community Assistance[7]

- **Coordinating Agency:** U.S. Department of Homeland Security (DHS) / FEMA
- **Mission:** Coordinate assistance and support from across the federal government and nongovernmental partners to help SLTTs effectively plan for and manage their recovery.
- **Strategic Outcomes:**
  - o Local government and community leaders have the knowledge, tools, and data needed to support their own recovery planning and strategy development, including community engagement, project identification and prioritization, and partnership development.
  - o Communities have a vision, plan, or process in place to support their long-term recovery goals and objectives.
  - o Communities and organizations are aware of potential funding sources for project implementation.

---

[6] FEMA, Recovery and Resilience Resource Library, 2024
[7] The Community Assistance RSF was formerly known as the Community Planning and Capacity Building RSF.

National Disaster Recovery Framework – Third Edition

- o Communities have access to the information and processes that allow them to recover in a sustainable, resilient, and inclusive manner.
- **Responsibilities:**
  - o Provide advice, guidance, and/or direct support to communities in the recovery planning processes.
  - o Support communities in identifying recovery priorities, goals, and milestones to achieve successful recovery and increase long-term resilience.
  - o Coordinate with affected community leaders to identify and provide tools and resources to address management and planning needs (e.g., technical assistance).
  - o Engage and build relationships with external partners, and facilitate coordination, communication, and information sharing across federal, SLTT, and nongovernmental partners to support community recovery planning and implementation of community recovery priorities.

> **RSF Structure in Action: Data-Driven Decision Making**
>
> Following Hurricanes Irma and María in September 2017, the Community Assistance RSF deployed to Puerto Rico. Community Assistance staff conducted a Community Conditions Assessment, which evaluated communities based on their capacity, vulnerability, and disaster impacts. Using this information, the Community Assistance RSF initiated a Community Recovery Mapping Project. This project provided technical assistance, training, and support to create a map which visualized the results of the Assessment. Communities used this data to access additional financial resources to serve their unmet recovery needs. This demonstrates how data-driven decision making ultimately creates better outcomes for communities post-disaster.

Economic

- **Coordinating Agency:** U.S. Department of Commerce (DOC) / Economic Development Administration (EDA)
- **Mission:** Integrate the expertise of the federal government to help SLTTs and their partners in sustaining and rebuilding businesses, revitalizing employment, and developing economic opportunities that result in sustainable, economically resilient communities after large-scale or catastrophic incidents.
- **Strategic Outcomes:**
  - o Disaster-impacted businesses are rapidly stabilized and receive the assistance needed to maintain operations and cover workforce payroll expenses.
  - o SLTTs and business and industry can effectively navigate and leverage federal economic recovery resources to support priority recovery projects.
  - o SLTTs, business and industry, and nongovernmental partners have increased capacity to develop and implement comprehensive economic recovery strategies that guide investment in new economic opportunities and enhance economic resilience.
  - o Communities have a greater understanding of future risks and vulnerabilities to consider in their economic planning.

- **Responsibilities:**
  - Support the capacity of SLTT partners, business and industry, and community members to develop and implement comprehensive economic recovery strategies.
  - Support the capacity of SLTT partners, business and industry, and community members to identify and mitigate pre-disaster vulnerabilities that may hinder economic recovery efforts and help communities plan for long- term resilience.
  - Facilitate federal interagency communication and collaboration during recovery to ensure the aligned investment of resources in support of SLTT economic recovery priorities.
  - Provide business owners with assistance that is critical to the continuity of operations, including access to capital as well as technical guidance, and promote early economic stabilization for business and industry partners.

RSF Structure in Action: Partners in Economic Recovery

Hurricane Idalia, a Category 3 storm, made landfall approximately 60 miles north of Cedar Key, Florida on August 30, 2023. The Florida Department of Agriculture and Consumer Services estimated that Florida shellfish and aquaculture processors saw more than $34.1 million in losses from Hurricane Idalia. A National Oceanic and Atmospheric Administration Sea Grant aquaculture extension specialist, working with the local growers' association, estimated that Hurricane Idalia impacted more than 80 percent of the clam industry in Cedar Key. This loss resulted in layoffs and workers placed on significantly reduced work schedules.

In September 2023, the Economic RSF met with the U.S. Department of Labor to discuss the impacts of the hurricane. This led to a series of strategic discussions between CareerSource Florida (state and local Department of Labor-supported workforce boards), Florida Sea Grant, and other state/federal partners. In February 2024, a project funded through the U.S. Department of Labor National Dislocated Worker Grant program was launched by the partners to help clam farmers and their dislocated workers get back to work. Between the start of the project and June 2024, a total of $6 million was invested. The local CareerSource Board credited the Economic RSF for playing a key role in helping this project come to fruition.

Health, Education, and Human Services[8]

- **Coordinating Agency:** U.S. Department of Health and Human Services (HHS) / Administration for Strategic Preparedness and Response (ASPR)
- **Mission:** Assist locally led recovery efforts to restore public health, health care, human services, education, and behavioral health networks to promote the resilience, health, and well-being of affected individuals and communities.
- **Strategic Outcomes:**
  - Health care, public health, environmental health, behavioral health, education, and human services systems operations that support individuals, families, and communities are restored in the affected area.
  - Enable K-12 schools and institutions of higher education to promptly resume instruction.
  - Communities prevent long-term student learning disruption due to displacement, emotional stresses of the post-disaster environment, and other developmental impacts to children and youth over the recovery period.

---

[8] The Health, Education, and Human Services RSF was formerly known as Health and Human Services RSF.

National Disaster Recovery Framework – Third Edition

- o Service providers are equipped to respond to future hazards and create more resilient and sustainable health care, public health, behavioral health, education, and human service systems.
- o Communities are prepared to address pre-disaster health and economic disparities to ensure rapid and equitably distributed recovery efforts.
- o Communities prevent or mitigate specific medical, psychosocial, developmental, and behavioral health harms to individuals and families that often occur during the prolonged post-disaster period.
- **Responsibilities:**
  - o Mitigate post-disaster stress for the affected community, provide additional coping and resilience skills support, maintain the behavioral health clinical workforce, and identify survivors that require clinical-level intervention.
  - o Restore and adapt health care systems across the spectrum of care services to meet community needs in the post-disaster environment and give disaster survivors access to health care services.
  - o Assess the post-disaster environment to effectively restore community public and nonprofit human services and adapt public health interventions to prevent cascading hazards during recovery.
  - o Provide and coordinate financial and technical resources, and assistance for K-12 schools and institutions of higher education recovering after a natural disaster, to adapt learning to the post-disaster environment and provide effective support for staff and students.
  - o Help communities rebuild in ways that promote public and environmental health and safety for individuals and families.

> **RSF Structure in Action: Building Public Health Capacity**
>
> In the aftermath of Super Typhoon Mawar in 2023, Guam public health officials recognized a critical need to enhance their management of various public health concerns, particularly mold mitigation and lead control. In response, the Health, Education, and Human Services RSF, led by the U.S. Centers for Disease Control and Prevention, deployed a specialized team of mold and lead experts to address the unique challenges faced by communities in Guam. These federal experts conducted a thorough assessment to identify specific local challenges and developed and delivered customized training sessions to Guam public health officials. These sessions were designed to build the public health capacity of Guam, equipping public health officials with the knowledge and skills needed to strengthen their internal public health capabilities and effectively manage mold and lead issues in the wake of the disaster.

Housing
- **Coordinating Agency:** U.S. Department of Housing and Urban Development (HUD)
- **Mission:** Provide housing development expertise while engaging in and facilitating collaboration among federal, state, local, and territorial partners involved in housing recovery. Support communities in developing a holistic, inclusive, and equitable recovery plan and implementation process. Assist in assessing impacts, determining key issues, analyzing damage data, and identifying resources, tools, and technical assistance to support the communities' resilient and sustainable rebuilding.

- **Strategic Outcomes:**
  - Communities have identified key long-term recovery considerations, implementation strategies and rebuilding priorities through partner engagement.
  - SLTTs and community recovery partners are aware of the resources, tools, and technical assistance available to affected communities along with their administrative, regulatory, and programmatic flexibilities available to affected communities.
  - Long-term recovery and rebuilding planning and implementation are built on a foundation of resilience, inclusion, fairness, information sharing, and coalition building.
  - Communities become more resilient and sustainable through data-driven recovery planning and implementation that examine all areas of impact and identify solutions.
  - Communities can enhance overall recovery capacity through a continuous process of assessment, improvement, and resource identification, and by embracing new and strengthening existing partnerships.
- **Responsibilities:**
  - Provide affected communities with support, guidance, impact and damage data, and other useful housing information to create a recovery plan.
  - Coordinate the delivery of training and technical assistance opportunities to enhance local capacity to identify long-term rebuilding priorities and recovery implementation strategies.
  - Collaborate with SLTTs and other recovery partners to identify necessary financial resources, tools, and technical assistance to support housing recovery planning.
  - Identify and engage partners to facilitate whole community inclusion and fairness in housing recovery planning.
  - Communicate to SLTTs the flexibilities and administrative, regulatory, and programmatic disaster relief available to affected communities.
  - Promote and assist coalition building, including information sharing to facilitate successful long-term housing recovery.

RSF Structure in Action: Housing Assessment and Resource Allocation

Following Hurricane María in Puerto Rico in 2017, the Housing RSF, in collaboration with other RSFs and various local and national organizations, conducted a comparative analysis of pre- and post-disaster housing stock and housing conditions. By gathering data from multiple sources, including an analysis of FEMA-verified loss data for both homeowners and renters, the Housing Impact Assessment summarized the hurricane's impacts and damages to housing. This assessment equipped the Commonwealth with actionable insights to support recovery planning for affected communities. Puerto Rico used the Assessment to develop its comprehensive Community Development Block Grant Disaster Recovery Action Plan, which secured an allocation of approximately $20 billion.

Infrastructure Systems

- **Coordinating Agency:** U.S. Department of Defense (DOD) / U.S. Army Corps of Engineers (USACE)
- **Mission:** Provide support to SLTTs undertaking the rehabilitation and reconstruction of affected infrastructure systems through coordinated delivery of federal resources, while supporting long-term infrastructure resilience that highlights the use of new, accessible, and permanent infrastructure system options.

National Disaster Recovery Framework – Third Edition

- **Strategic Outcomes:**
  - SLTTs and business and industry partners receive technical assistance that supports infrastructure systems restoration (primarily energy, water/wastewater, transportation, communications, and watershed management) while working toward strengthening system resilience.
  - SLTT and community leaders are informed about existing federal programs, authorities, and available funding that support long-term infrastructure recovery, resilience planning, and project implementation.
  - SLTTs and communities have the resources and support to visualize and develop plans for future projects that use available sustainable/resilient infrastructure technologies, methods, and materials.
  - SLTT and community leaders have the information and data necessary to identify and prioritize infrastructure recovery needs, any associated recovery costs, and an understanding of federal processes to address infrastructure recovery needs.

- **Responsibilities:**
  - Coordinate federal support to help restore infrastructure systems and services while advancing resilient options that enable infrastructure systems to withstand and quickly recover from future disaster events.
  - Support SLTT infrastructure system recovery and redevelopment through technical assistance and guidance, including resiliency strategies that consider and respect cultural and community concerns.
  - Inform SLTT and communities about federal program eligibility, application processes, and project requirements through information sharing and technical assistance.
  - Help communities envision and plan more resilient and viable infrastructure that considers impacts from the changing environment and uses new, efficient, and green technologies.
  - Enhance a community's ability to identify, mitigate, and recover from impacts to infrastructure systems by addressing additional disaster-dependent concerns such as environmental issues, aging infrastructure system failures, adopting modern building codes, providing sufficient energy to operate modern systems, and cybersecurity system gaps.

> **RSF Structure in Action: Enhancing Recovery for Remote Communities After Typhoon Merbok**
>
> In September of 2022, Typhoon Merbok impacted 1,300 miles of the Alaskan coastline, including more than 60 Alaska Native Villages and municipalities. The infrastructure impacts were widespread, affecting erosion control, water and wastewater systems, solid waste disposal, energy infrastructure, and more. The Infrastructure Systems RSF led coordinated efforts to enhance resilience and support recovery across the impacted communities by collaborating with multiple partners. Working with the Bureau of Indian Affairs, the Infrastructure Systems RSF launched a quarry development initiative designed to benefit impacted Alaska Native Villages. This collaboration also addressed critical infrastructure needs such as securing funding for new fuel storage tanks. By working closely with the U.S. Department of Transportation's Maritime Administration, the Infrastructure Systems RSF promoted the use of Port Infrastructure Development Program grants to improve community landings in 22 locations, facilitating better access to essential goods and services. They also provided vital hazard mitigation planning guidance and collaborated with the Alaska Department of Transportation to plan more resilient barge landings across the affected areas.

Natural and Cultural Resources

- **Coordinating Agency:** U.S. Department of the Interior (DOI)
- **Mission:** Assist SLTTs in the protection, preservation, and recovery of natural and cultural resources after disaster. Natural resources are land, fish, wildlife, biota, air, and water. Cultural resources are tangible entities or cultural practices that represent the diverse history, art, and traditions of our nation.
- **Strategic Outcomes:**
  - Communities are equipped to conduct pre- and post-disaster recovery planning for Natural and Cultural Resources in alignment with federal priorities.
  - Time-critical actions have been taken to stabilize affected natural, cultural, artistic, and historic resources, and SLTT partners have an implementable strategy in place to address long-term restoration, rehabilitation, conservation, and preservation needs according to community priorities. This can include sources of potential funding or technical assistance for identified projects.
  - Emergency and long-term actions comply with applicable laws and regulations and have been informed by cultural literacy, the best available science, and proven management practices to support an equitable, sustainable, and resilient recovery.
- **Responsibilities:**
  - Facilitate technical assistance and resources from various federal, SLTT, nongovernmental organization (NGO), and private sources to support the protection, preservation, and recovery of natural and cultural resources.
  - Conduct education and outreach at the federal and SLTT levels to mitigate future damage to natural and cultural resources.
  - Assist SLTT agencies and community organizations with plan development to ensure long-term resilience of natural and cultural resources. Plans shall focus on the integration of adaptation and mitigation methods based on the best available science, applicable environmental laws, executive orders, guidelines, and best management practices.
  - Assess impacts on natural and cultural resources in the disaster-impacted area by coordinating with response personnel.
  - Identify protections that should be present during stabilization through recovery which foster and preserve the potential for rehabilitation and restoration.
  - Develop a timeline that considers available natural and budgetary resources for addressing efforts to repair and restore natural and cultural resources in a sustainable and resilient manner.
  - Enhance the capacity of practitioners, tradespersons, and artists necessary to implement recovery projects.
  - Jointly develop infrastructure and ecosystem restoration plans.
  - Preserve and restore natural and cultural resources as part of an overall community recovery that is achieved through the coordinated efforts of subject-matter experts and the recovery team in accordance with the specified timeline in the recovery plan.

National Disaster Recovery Framework – Third Edition

> **RSF Structure in Action: Integrating Recovery and Mitigation for Coral Reef Protection**
>
> The 2017 hurricane season caused major damage to Puerto Rico's coral reefs. To repair the damage, the Natural and Cultural Resources RSF collaborated with FEMA, the National Oceanic and Atmospheric Administration (NOAA), and the Puerto Rico Department of Natural and Environmental Resources to assess reef damage and initiate restoration efforts. With FEMA funding, NOAA led the emergency reattachment of approximately 16,000 corals across 63 sites in Puerto Rico.[9]
>
> Under the Natural and Cultural Resources RSF, NOAA also provided technical assistance for ongoing restoration planning, resulting in FEMA's first-ever natural resource restoration project through the Hazard Mitigation Grant Program (HMGP). This $38.6 million project will enhance the coral reef system one kilometer offshore of San Juan, utilizing a hybrid gray-green design with coral outplanting to reduce flooding and protect around 800 structures in nearby communities, including Condado, Ocean Park, and Puntas Las Marías.[10]

NATIONAL COORDINATORS

Each of the six Federal RSFs is led by a Coordinating Agency, with a designated National Coordinator, who is a senior staff member. The National Coordinator manages the Coordinating Agency's roles and responsibilities within the RSF while aligning interagency partners efforts. Additionally, the National Coordinator engages all participating agencies and organizations within the RSF to ensure successful mission delivery. Key National Coordinator responsibilities include:

- Facilitating collaboration, coordination, and effective communication among all RSF participating agencies and organizations to achieve stated goals.
- Exploring opportunities for utilizing applicable funding and programs across the RSF (steady state or disaster-specific) to facilitate recovery.
- Training and educating staff, including individuals who may deploy to support recovery activities, across the RSF's participating agencies and organizations to deliver operational support in the mission area.
- Informing national disaster recovery and resilience policy and program development.
- Incorporating lessons learned from previous field operations to continuously improve recovery strategies.

Post-disaster, National Coordinator responsibilities include:

- Designating the RSF Field Coordinator and other mission support team members.
- Coordinating the involvement of participating agencies and organizations based on mission requirements identified by the FDRO, in collaboration with the Field Coordinator and/or as requested by SLTTs.
- Ensuring collaboration with regional points of contact of the RSF participating agencies and organizations to gain local context, connect with local networks, and ensure long-term continuity.
- Identifying steady state or disaster funding programs available from their agency as well as other agencies to support community needs and operations.

---

[9] National Oceanic and Atmospheric Administration, Post-Disaster Coral Reef Assessment and Restoration Set Important Precedent for Coastal Communities, 2020
[10] FEMA, FEMA Allocates Millions to Restore coral Reefs in the Coast of San Juan, 2023.

- Establishing and accepting Mission Assignments with FEMA, including Mission Assignment extensions, Interagency Reimbursable Work Agreements (IRWAs),[11] or Interagency Agreements (IAAs)[12] for a recovery activation when appropriate. Mission Assignments may also be established directly with a Participating Agency, organization, or other federal agency based on identified disaster recovery needs.[13]

- Training and supporting Field Coordinators for the development of mission activities and deliverables, such as Recovery Needs Assessments, community engagement, and/or Recovery Support Strategy.

- Liaising with leadership to ensure RSF efforts are aligned with the overall recovery strategy.

RECOVERY SUPPORT FUNCTION FIELD COORDINATORS

The RSF's National Coordinator designates each RSF Field Coordinator to serve as the senior mission-specific operational lead for each RSF Mission Assignment. Key Field Coordinator responsibilities include:

- Managing the deployed federal interagency personnel of their agency and other agencies activated to support the RSF mission.

- Maintaining accountability of federal and contractor assets deployed in support of the RSF.

- Promoting new and reinforcing existing relationships between federal and SLTT partners.

- Identifying and documenting key community recovery needs and challenges in a Recovery Needs Assessment, and managing its preparation, along with the Recovery Support Strategy, for submission to FEMA operational leadership and SLTT authorities.

- Liaising with leadership on behalf of the Coordinating Agency and with the other RSF participating agencies and organizations.

- Focusing federal resources on the most pertinent recovery needs.

ADVISORS

Participating agencies and organizations can activate field-level advisors who are subject-matter experts with extensive knowledge of how department or agency resources align with community recovery needs. Advisors support tasks related to sustainability, agriculture, disability integration, civil rights compliance, mitigation, Unified Federal Environmental and Historic Preservation Review resources, academia, and philanthropy among other topics. They may also represent department and agency equities such as rural development and water systems. Advisors assist the FCO, FDRC, FDRO, and/or Field Coordinators develop locally and regionally appropriate recovery strategies. Their unique skillset and expertise can help leadership and staff identify solutions that meet incident-level needs.

---

[11] U.S. Department of Homeland Security, Homeland Security Acquisition Manual Subchapter 3017.5 Interagency Acquisitions, 2021
[12] U.S. Department of Homeland Security, Homeland Security Acquisition Manual Subchapter 3017.5 Interagency Acquisitions, 2021
[13] Participating agencies and organizations can provide recovery support through multiple avenues, including their normal authorities, steady state programs, and existing relationships.

National Disaster Recovery Framework – Third Edition

4. State, Local, Tribal Nation, and Territorial Roles and Responsibilities

SLTTs play a critical role in disaster recovery, relying on their own capacities and authorities to lead recovery for most disasters. While the federal government provides resources, expertise, and additional support, SLTTs are responsible for organizing and executing recovery within their communities. This includes disaster recovery practitioners who may also support recovery work on an as-needed basis. For example, a school superintendent may be designated as their community's disaster recovery lead for education and social services.

To effectively manage recovery efforts, there are several best practices SLTTs can implement to be better positioned to recover from a disaster.

Best practices to consider implementing **pre-disaster** include:

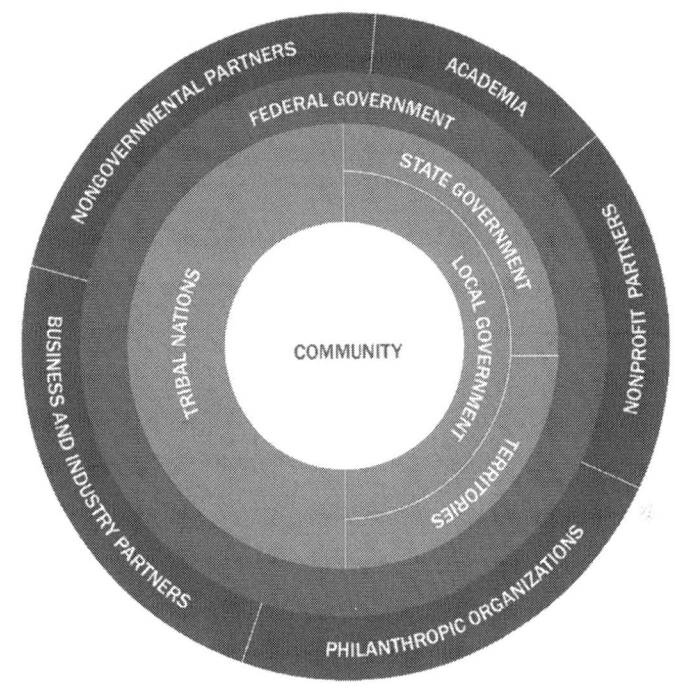

Figure 3: Community-Driven Recovery
Community-Driven Recovery depicts local communities at the center of any disaster recovery. Federal and non-federal partners organize their support

- Identify the government entity and position responsible for leading recovery coordination, as well as the individuals who will act as liaisons between governmental entities and NGOs. This includes the respective SLTT disaster recovery coordinators. Some commonly used positions include the Local Disaster Recovery Manager (LDRM), State Disaster Recovery Coordinator (SDRC), Territorial Disaster Recovery Coordinator (TDRC), and Tribal Disaster Recovery Coordinator (Tribal DRC).

- Identify who else within the government or community at large needs to be involved and determine a coordination structure (e.g., key positions, offices). Depending on the scale of the impact, these individuals may concurrently support recovery and ongoing emergency response efforts.

- Develop, adopt, and maintain pre-disaster recovery and resilience assessments and plans.

- Develop an engagement and communication plan that includes and considers historically marginalized or underserved communities[14] as well as neighboring jurisdictions and Tribal Nations.

- Identify and develop strong relationships and networks with SLTT recovery counterparts, as well as nonprofit, philanthropic, and business and industry partners, to determine what types of assistance may be available post-disaster and document important information. This includes priorities, roles, responsibilities, resources, communication channels, and tasks.

---

[14] FEMA, Achieving Equitable Recovery, 2023

- Establish memorandums of understanding (MOU) and mechanisms to ensure adequate resources are available post-disaster, including coordination with nonprofit and philanthropic partners as well as for-profit and nonprofit disability service providers.
- Conduct training and exercises regularly to educate recovery partners and ensure effective coordination pre- and post-disaster (e.g., Stafford Act processes and resources for Elected Officials).
- Determine data needs and collection mechanisms (e.g., information required to conduct or inform damage assessments to include for Stafford Act Declarations or other agency programs).
- Develop identifiable metrics for successful recovery from pre-identified threats, based on appropriate Threat and Hazard Identification and Risk Assessment (THIRA)/Stakeholder Preparedness Report (SPR), and other resources that can help jurisdictions understand their risks and inform mitigation strategies, such as State Energy Security Plans.
- Develop partnerships and conduct pre-disaster coordination and planning opportunities with business and industry leaders to include procurement and mutual disaster exercises.

Post-disaster actions enable communities to establish and refine recovery priorities, goals, and objectives, identify specific projects in areas of critical importance, and identify opportunities to improve community resilience against threats and hazards.

Best practices to consider implementing **post-disaster recovery** include:

- Assign disaster-specific individuals to lead coordination between states, Tribal Nations, territories, and/or federal agencies and NGOs. This includes the LDRM, and the SDRC, TDRC, or Tribal DRC.
- Initiate and coordinate recovery activities as community lifelines stabilize through SLTT coordination structures.
- Conduct initial damage assessments to inform recovery planning and potential federal requests for assistance.
- Establish a communications structure to share information internally and externally, ensuring that communications are accessible to all communities.
- Maintain communications with business and industry partners about operations and supply chain status, as well as restoration challenges and timelines.
- Conduct outreach and listening sessions to understand community needs, being mindful of survivors' suffering, and including means of access and representation from the whole community.
- Set resilient recovery priorities and outcomes in partnership with affected communities focusing on sustainable and inclusive outcomes.
- Develop a disaster recovery plan that promotes local decision-making and ownership as it ultimately becomes the roadmap for all levels of government and nongovernmental partners to provide resources and support. Disaster recovery plans should be updated as needed and adjusted based on continuing information analysis.
- Develop and maintain an accessible system to manage and monitor progress made toward recovery goals and project implementation.
- Engage governmental and nongovernmental partners to identify and determine how to cover unmet needs.
- Implement MOUs and other agreements to facilitate effective post-disaster coordination.

> **Post-disaster Recovery Planning: Turning Losses into Lessons**
>
> In 2017, the Tubbs Fire ravaged Santa Rosa, California. Despite having adopted its hazard mitigation plan in 2016, the city quickly recognized the need to update the plan after the fire claimed 24 lives and destroyed more than 3,000 homes. Santa Rosa successfully secured funding through the FEMA Hazard Mitigation Grant Program (HMGP) and the city's fire department led a citywide effort to develop a community wildfire protection plan as an annex to the existing hazard mitigation plan. This annex provided detailed wildfire risk assessments, prioritized risk reduction in planning, and offered homeowners guidance to protect their properties.

4.1. Local Governments

Local governments are responsible for adopting and implementing recovery strategies because they directly represent the interests and needs of the affected community. Depending on the type and severity of a disaster, local governments may receive support from the federal government, states, Tribal Nations, or territories, as well as neighboring municipalities and regional authorities. Even with this support, local governments may face and need to plan for capacity constraints when responding to and recovering from disasters (e.g., insufficient staff, limited recovery and resilience subject-matter expertise).

In the wake of disasters, local officials and public employees may need to assume disaster recovery-related roles and responsibilities beyond their regular duties. Recovery is often the responsibility of many departments, extending beyond emergency management professionals to those involved in affected sectors (e.g., education or business leaders when schools or local businesses have been damaged or destroyed). This may require additional community engagement and coordination, preparing and submitting grant applications, and other functions. It is also important to consider that many of these individuals may need to manage disaster recovery work while also suffering from and dealing with personal loss caused by the disaster.

Local governments can build their capacity and resilience before a disaster (e.g., providing trainings for staff, hardening infrastructure). These actions involve balancing observable physical, environmental, and societal risks with corresponding mitigation strategies. This includes establishing local recovery policies and methods to formally coordinate the solicitation and consideration of input from across the whole community.

4.2. States and Territories

States and territories play a critical role in coordinating disaster recovery efforts. They may serve as the conduit for federal support to local communities, Tribal Nations, NGOs, and business and industry partners. It is critical for states and territories to establish and maintain clear and open lines of communication with all disaster recovery partners. It is also important to note that management roles, authorities, and capabilities essential for effective disaster recovery do not reside exclusively within a state or territory emergency management structure. While emergency managers may often lead coordination, successful disaster recovery involves all departments and agencies engaging and committing staff to supporting recovery efforts (e.g., housing or economic recovery).

States or territories may choose to adopt their own disaster recovery framework that parallels the federal RSF structure. The structure and functions of state or territory RSFs can vary based on factors such as capacity, staffing, funding, frequency of events, and other considerations. Due to the variety of state and territorial structures and functions, it is the responsibility of the federal RSFs to strategically align with the state or territory's recovery structure to effectively provide recovery support.

National Disaster Recovery Framework – Third Edition

> **Pre-Disaster Housing Initiative: Seizing the Opportunity to Plan Ahead**
>
> Planning for a disaster housing mission can be an enormous challenge. In 2023, FEMA and HUD undertook a first-of-its-kind initiative to bring emergency managers and housing officials together to prepare for resilient disaster housing recovery. The pilot program included Louisiana, Montana, New Jersey, and Washington as the first cohort. Over seven months, the states worked with housing and recovery subject-matter experts to build relationships, address challenges, and create housing recovery strategies that leveraged the resources and expertise of both FEMA and HUD. By connecting these key players before a disaster, the program enabled more effective support for survivors and local communities as they transition from recovery into rebuilding.

4.3. Tribal Nations

As sovereign nations, Tribal Nations take the lead in preparing for and managing their disaster recovery efforts. Tribal Nations are often the first and sometimes only responders to disasters within their communities.[15] While Tribal Nations are constantly innovating as they prepare for and recover from disasters, they also rely on the traditional ecological knowledge and nature-based solutions that have effectively promoted resilient disaster recovery for centuries.

Tribal communities may include Tribal citizens residing within and beyond the Tribal Nation's jurisdictional boundaries, as well as descendants of the Tribal Nation, Tribal Nation employees, and non-Tribal Nation members or non-natives living within the Tribal Nation. The federal government has a trust and treaty responsibility[16] to Tribal Nations, each of which faces unique circumstances and challenges. The disaster recovery needs of individual Tribal Nations are driven by their distinct and varying political structures, cultures, religions, and historical contexts, among many other factors. While Tribal Nations may consider utilizing the federal RSF structure to develop and adopt their own disaster recovery framework, it is the responsibility of the federal RSFs to align with the Tribal Nation's recovery structure to effectively provide recovery support.

> **Planning for Your Neighbor: Culturally Competent Language for Working with Tribal Nations**
>
> It is critical for all disaster recovery partners to understand that Tribal Nations may have religious and/or cultural beliefs that guide how they manage disasters, including the use of appropriate language surrounding disasters, death, and recovery. These important considerations are vital to maintaining positive relationships with Tribal Nations. Failure to do so can erode trust, sometimes with long-lasting consequences including shutting the door on working with that Tribal Nation.
>
> For example, certain Tribal Nations may not speak about or plan for disasters as they believe this will bring disaster to their community. To engage in disaster recovery planning, some Tribal Nations have created plans for their neighbors, rather than themselves. It still requires Tribal Nations to work through the process, while the language they use is focused on planning for their neighbor.

---

[15] For information on how Tribal Nations may receive federal disaster recovery support, see Tribal Declarations Interim Guidance | FEMA.gov

[16] The federal Indian trust responsibility is a legal obligation under which the United States "has charged itself with moral obligations of the highest responsibility and trust" toward Indian Tribes (Seminole Nation v. United States, 316 U.S. 286, 297 [1942]). Over the years, the trust doctrine has been at the center of numerous other Supreme Court cases, thus making it one of the most important principles in federal Indian law. The federal Indian trust responsibility is also a legally enforceable fiduciary obligation on the part of the United States to protect Tribal treaty rights, lands, assets, and resources, as well as a duty to carry out the mandates of federal law with respect to American Indian and Alaska Native Tribes and Villages.

> **A Coordinated Recovery Effort: Partnerships in Remote Places**
>
> In western Alaska, coastal erosion, flooding, and permafrost degradation – largely due to environmental changes – threaten over 40 Alaska Native Villages reliant on subsistence livelihoods. These issues were worsened by Typhoon Merbok in 2022. In the wake of this disaster the Community Assistance RSF provided recovery management technical assistance to 12 Alaska Native Villages due to the area's extreme remoteness, limited infrastructure, and vulnerability. The Community Assistance RSF facilitated recovery coordination among the complex governance structures of these ~500-resident communities, including working with city and Tribal Councils and Village Corporations, and bringing in various agencies and partners for support. Erosion protection was identified as a high priority, leading the Community Assistance RSF and the Infrastructure Systems RSF to help communities apply for a pilot program with no local cost match, resulting in six applications. Additionally, the Community Assistance RSF supported Alaska Native Villages in applying for Bureau of Indian Affairs disaster supplemental funding, resulting in nine applications and securing $25 million for home repairs and subsistence equipment replacement.

5. Nongovernmental Resources

Disaster affected communities and survivors may have needs greater than the assistance available from the federal government and SLTTs. Nongovernmental partners, such as Long-Term Recovery Groups (LTRG), NGOs, philanthropic organizations, business and industry entities, as well as academic institutions can often address ongoing or unmet community needs using their resources, capabilities, and donations. While the availability of these resources may vary by geography and circumstances, they provide essential support in many forms. Community members and SLTT officials should actively incorporate these options into their pre- and post-disaster recovery plans.

SLTTs should leverage their existing relationships with nongovernmental partners to enhance disaster recovery efforts. Partners that collaborate during normal circumstances are often well-positioned to quickly step in to provide disaster recovery assistance such as funding, human resources, and strategic guidance. By drawing on these established connections, communities can recover from disasters more quickly and build resilience against future challenges. This approach fosters a more sustainable recovery process by leveraging the strengths and capabilities of diverse sectors to support community well-being and resilience.

5.1. Long-Term Recovery Groups

Following a disaster, community-based organizations and partners may choose to form a single unified group through which members organize their recovery operations. This unified group is often called an LTRG, whose goal is to match recovery resources with community needs to ensure that even the most vulnerable in the community can recover from the disaster.

LTRGs can include community leaders, local NGOs, Voluntary Organizations Active in Disasters (VOADs), state and federal government representatives, community-wide and neighborhood leaders, business and industry partners, disability organizations, faith-based leaders, and other recovery partners. FEMA Voluntary Agency Liaisons (VALs), are often involved and establish supportive long-term relationships with members of the LTRG.

By including community-based partners that routinely utilize volunteers in their work, LTRGs are better equipped to recruit and coordinate volunteers. They can efficiently handle an influx of inquiries from people eager to donate their time, but who are unsure of how to get involved, matching them with the appropriate organizations ready to utilize volunteers for recovery efforts. This is essential as volunteer support is critical to many organizations after a disaster when the need for their services often exceeds their regular capacity.

LTRGs are usually established for a specific incident and are not intended to be permanent. They may last for a few months or a few years depending on community needs but usually disband once the affected community has reached established key recovery milestones. The specific functions and priorities that an LTRG serves may vary by disaster as they are dependent on the unique characteristics of the community, group leadership, and committee members.

> **Impacts of a Community Long-Term Recovery Group: Healing Past Wounds**
>
> LTRGs play a vital role in recovery efforts by empowering communities to identify their needs and coordinating assistance. After the Marshall Fire and Windstorm in Boulder, Colorado, the "Marshall Restoring Our Community" LTRG built trusted relationships with survivors and supporting agencies. The group united resources and centered survivors' needs, opening the Marshall Fire Recovery Center to provide services such as mental health support and community connection. The LTRG worked closely with social services agencies and disaster case management to address critical unmet needs like food insecurity and mental health services. In October 2023, the LTRG organized a Multi-Agency Recovery Center event called "Marshall Fire Moving Forward," bringing together 400 survivors and 35 agencies to help identify resource gaps and build relationships. Their smoke and ash task force exemplifies their ability to adapt and coordinate resources to meet evolving local recovery goals.

5.2. Nongovernmental Organizations

NGOs are independent, not-for-profit entities that work for the public good. The capacity of a nongovernmental organization[17] can range from small community-based nonprofits to national organizations with extensive experience in disaster response and recovery.

NGOs have access to recovery-related knowledge, skills, and resources that can be used to help communities pre- and post-disaster. Many NGOs maintain existing relationships with other disaster recovery partners and may help contribute to SLTT preparedness and planning efforts. During disaster recovery, NGOs often take the lead on a multitude of needs that SLTT and federal partners may not have the capacity to address. These critical partners can support recovery through:

- Crisis Counseling (i.e., behavioral health)
- Casework and Case Management
- Legal Services (i.e., succession deeds, fair housing, insurance)
- Disaster Unemployment Assistance
- Emergency Food and Shelter
- Transitional Sheltering Assistance
- Direct Housing
- Mass Care
- Disability Services
- Volunteer and Donations Management
- Animal Care and Sheltering
- Training and Technical Assistance
- Funding Resources and Grants
- Cleanup and Debris Removal
- Mold Remediation
- Distribution of Emergency Supplies
- Construction (i.e., major and minor home repairs, mitigation efforts, reconstruction)
- Financial and Insurance Literacy
- Long-Term Recovery Coordination
- Advocacy
- Community Development

---

[17] NGOs include VOADs and other nonprofits, encompassing voluntary, faith- and community-based, business and industry, philanthropic, minority or disability-focused groups, and whole community partners who help individuals and communities equitably plan for, respond to, and recover from disasters.

NGOs are vital partners in disaster management, bridging gaps and addressing immediate needs while laying the groundwork for recovery and resilience. Their diverse roles enhance the collective humanitarian response to disasters. NGOs often originate from or remain in disaster-affected communities and can continue to mobilize and provide recovery support to individuals and the community. As such, it is crucial that NGOs receive timely information from and closely coordinate with their SLTT counterparts.

5.3. Philanthropy, Business and Industry, and Academia

In addition to LTRG, VOAD, and NGO resources, disaster recovery resources may also be available from other non-federal partners such as philanthropy, business and industry, and academia. Engaging philanthropic organizations can unlock grants, donations, and expertise dedicated to supporting communities in times of need. Business and industry partnerships can bring in resources through corporate social responsibility initiatives, separate supply chains, and technical expertise, offering both immediate relief and long-term solutions. Academic institutions can contribute research, technical assistance, and innovative approaches to recovery and resilience.

PHILANTHROPY

Philanthropic organizations across the nation work to support disaster-affected SLTTs and survivors. This includes philanthropic partners at all levels, from organizations supporting disaster recovery nationwide down to local, community-specific aid groups and community foundations. Community foundations, in particular, can play a vital role by leveraging local knowledge and networks to address specific recovery needs. They may provide grants to nonprofits, rapidly mobilize donations and resources, and foster collaboration among recovery partners. These partners may fill recovery gaps a community has been unable to address or provide disaster survivors with additional financial aid to cover unmet needs.

Many RSF partners recognize the value of these contributions and have designated philanthropic liaisons to connect potential philanthropic partners with recovery initiatives for a coordinated and effective response. This can help communities recover and rebuild more quickly.

BUSINESS AND INDUSTRY

From Fortune 500 corporations to critical infrastructure owners and operators to small businesses and farms across the nation, business and industry partners in the private sector can play a key role in disaster recovery as partners in the whole community. These partners contribute significantly to the overall effectiveness of a community's resilience and recovery by ensuring the continuity of essential services and the stability of local economies. They also support recovery at every level of government by providing essential commodities, labor, and expertise through contract support. Their engagement and support are critical to the resilience and recovery of disaster-affected areas.

Business and industry own and operate the vast majority of the nation's critical infrastructure systems, such as electric power and financial and telecommunications systems, as well as the commodities, labor, and expertise required to recover from disasters. Accordingly, in order for a community to effectively recover, government and community leaders must effectively coordinate and communicate with business and industry.

Additionally, given their critical role, businesses are strongly encouraged to develop pre- and post-disaster recovery plans to ensure their continuity as well as support for their community's overall recovery. For example, businesses in critical infrastructure sectors such as water, power, telecommunications, and transportation can provide material and technical assistance to restore critical infrastructure affected by disasters through mutual aid and assistance. Restoring these services contributes to the immediate safety and well-being of communities and bolsters the operational capacity of other sectors. Similarly, the healthcare and pharmaceutical industries can ensure the availability of necessary medical supplies and services, while the retail and food industries can help meet basic consumer needs.

Small businesses and farms are of key importance both in providing jobs and in shaping the character and culture of a community. Disruptions due to disasters can result in families losing access to essential services and resources and destabilize local economies. The recovery and resilience of these businesses are essential to the overall health of the community. Involving business and industry partners in recovery planning and execution can bring innovative solutions and resources, enhancing the community's ability to bounce back from disasters.

> **Business Preparedness Resources: Locally Provided at No Cost**
>
> The Small Business Administration (SBA) Small Business Development Center (SBDC) Program helps businesses prepare for and recover from disasters. Through this program, small businesses can find resources and guidance for their preparedness, continuity planning, and disaster recovery. These services are delivered through individual SBDCs, local centers that collaborate with federal, state, and local disaster assistance providers within their communities. When disaster strikes, businesses can turn to their local SBDC for the help they need to recover. Business consultants at SBDCs offer no cost consulting aimed at minimizing losses and enhancing the survivability of businesses affected by disasters. These specialists can guide businesses through the process of applying for SBA and other federal and state disaster loans, offering step-by-step assistance to help them get back on their feet. SBA's network of resource partners, including its SBDCs, provide a wide range of services, including continuity planning to prevent business interruptions and financial guidance to help companies manage their finances and access emergency funds. These services are provided at no cost, ensuring that businesses have the resources they need to navigate through challenging times. More information can be found at sba.gov.

ACADEMIA

Academia can play a pivotal role in community recovery. Institutions of higher education offer a wide array of subject-matter expertise and specialized resources that can assist SLTTs with disaster recovery planning, mitigation, and resilience. Their expertise in fields like urban planning, environmental science, and engineering can inform effective recovery strategies.

Academic institutions can also develop and apply new technologies and innovative solutions to address challenges such as advanced mapping techniques, building resilient infrastructure, and creating sustainable recovery plans. For example, the nation's 111 public land-grant institutions, established to support agricultural sciences and engineering research, have partnered on a range of disaster recovery efforts highlighting academia's contribution to community recovery. Their trusted positions,

> **The Role of Think Tanks and Research Labs in Disaster Recovery**
>
> Think tanks and research laboratories play a crucial role in enhancing disaster recovery efforts. These organizations contribute through in-depth research, data analysis, and policy recommendations that inform recovery strategies and improve outcomes for affected communities. Through advanced analytical tools, predictive models, and innovative technologies, they support evidence-based decision making and optimize resource allocation. Think tanks also publish best practices and convene partners to foster collaboration and streamline recovery initiatives. Together, these entities drive innovation and provide valuable expertise, helping communities rebuild effectively and become more resilient to future disasters.

particularly in health sciences and education, help effectively engage diverse communities. Historically Black Colleges and Universities in particular maintain strong partnerships with African American communities across the country.

By leveraging these partnerships and resources, communities can ensure a more effective and sustainable rebuilding process after a disaster, leading to resilience and long-term recovery.

> **Leaning on Academia for Innovative Solutions**
>
> After Hurricane Michael struck Florida in 2018, many communities needed specialized assistance to recover. The Interagency Recovery Coordination group, sensing this need, identified a diverse array of experts, including the Infrastructure Systems RSF, a Sustainability Advisor from the Environmental Protection Agency (EPA), and the EPA Colleges/Underserved Community Partnership Program. This team leveraged multi-disciplinary engineering support from the Florida A&M University-Florida State University College of Engineering and the Drexel University College of Engineering to design a Dual Use Engineering Center. This initiative exemplified the NDRF's principle of integrating diverse expertise to achieve sustainable and innovative recovery solutions. By bringing together a wide range of skills and perspectives, the team also developed a cutting-edge facility that not only addressed immediate recovery needs but also provided long-term benefits for the community.

6. Conclusion

The NDRF serves as a guide, outlining the roles and responsibilities of federal, SLTT, nongovernmental, and private organizations involved in disaster recovery. While it provides a framework for how the federal government engages in recovery, it also acknowledges that SLTTs simultaneously lead their own response and recovery efforts. The NDRF emphasizes that recovery is most successful when it is organized around community-driven and locally defined goals. It promotes outcomes that are inclusive and sustainable, recognizing the importance of meeting the diverse needs of all community members and ensuring long-term success in recovery efforts. During both pre- and post-disaster recovery, the NDRF provides SLTTs with valuable information to inform and enhance their own disaster recovery efforts.

More importantly, the NDRF is not prescriptive. Instead, it serves as a flexible framework for SLTTs to effectively address the dynamic and evolving nature of disaster recovery, ultimately fostering stronger and more resilient communities. By using the NDRF, SLTTs can better prepare for and respond to these challenges, ensuring that their communities are more resilient and better equipped for future disasters. The NDRF stands as a critical resource for disaster recovery, advocating for community-focused approaches that prioritize inclusion, sustainability, whole community fairness, and resilience.

National Disaster Recovery Framework – Third Edition

Appendix A: Recovery Support Functions and Participating Agencies and Organizations

Appendix A contains RSF Fact Sheets (beginning on the next page) which include high-level summaries of what assistance the federal RSFs provide.

Federal Recovery Support Functions	Coordinating Agency
Community Assistance	U.S. Department of Homeland Security, Federal Emergency Management Agency
Economic	U.S. Department of Commerce, Economic Development Administration
Health, Education, and Human Services	U.S. Department of Health and Human Services, Administration for Strategic Preparedness and Response
Housing	U.S. Department of Housing and Urban Development
Infrastructure Systems	U.S. Department of Defense, U.S. Army Corps of Engineers
Natural and Cultural Resources	U.S. Department of the Interior

COMMUNITY ASSISTANCE RECOVERY SUPPORT FUNCTION

COORDINATING AGENCY: U.S. DEPARTMENT OF HOMELAND SECURITY, FEDERAL EMERGENCY MANAGEMENT AGENCY

MISSION

Coordinate assistance and support from across the federal government and nongovernmental partners to help state, local, Tribal Nation, and territorial governments (SLTTs) effectively plan for and manage their recovery.

BEFORE A DISASTER

BUILDING CAPACITY

- Promote collaborative approaches to disaster housing recovery and bolster SLTT capacity to develop pre-disaster housing recovery plans.
  Example: Leading FEMA's participation and support of the Pre-Disaster Housing Initiative (PDHI) to help states identify and address pre-existing housing issues to expedite housing recovery.

PARTNERSHIP DEVELOPMENT

- Identify, connect, and coordinate federal, SLTT, and nongovernmental partners and resources.
  Example: Hosting the Colorado United recovery symposium in federal/state partnership to share lessons learned, build local partnerships, identify resources and bring together community leaders.
- Conduct outreach on Community Assistance Recovery Support Function offerings and capabilities.

PLANNING AND PREPAREDNESS

- Support the development of SLTT pre- and post-disaster recovery plans and capacity.
- Example: Issuing pre-disaster recovery planning guides for Tribal Nation, state, and local partners.

TECHNICAL ASSISTANCE, TOOLS, AND TRAINING

- Develop tools and materials for SLTTs to utilize in planning, managing and leading their recovery.
  Example: The Community Recovery Management Toolkit.

AFTER A DISASTER

BUILDING CAPACITY

- Assist SLTTs with identifying management needs and resources.

COMMUNITY ASSISTANCE RECOVERY SUPPORT FUNCTION

COORDINATING AGENCY: U.S. DEPARTMENT OF HOMELAND SECURITY, FEDERAL EMERGENCY MANAGEMENT AGENCY

AFTER A DISASTER (CONT.)

PARTNERSHIP DEVELOPMENT

- Provide connections to peer mentors, advisors, and networks for community recovery advice and guidance from experienced leaders.
  Example: Utilizing peer connections to current and prior community leaders to bring lessons and experience from their disaster recovery.

- Promote equitable and inclusive recovery.
  Example: Providing resources, such as the recent Achieving Equitable Recovery guide, to inform SLTT leaders and officials.

- Conduct public engagement and outreach, such as resource fairs, community meetings, conferences, and public forums.
  Example: Supporting agricultural and farm recovery renters, hosting community listening sessions, and supporting housing and other issue area resource fairs.

PLANNING AND PREPAREDNESS

- Facilitate community visioning sessions for long-term resilient recovery.
  Example: Assisting communities with developing action-oriented recovery plans, with specific implementation steps and project goals.

- Support outreach and engagement of the whole community in the recovery planning process.
  Example: Facilitating community engagement in coordination with community leaders, and preparing community engagement summary reports.

TECHNICAL ASSISTANCE, TOOLS, AND TRAINING

- Provide planning technical assistance, direct support, and / or guidance, and assist SLTTs with identifying potential funding and resources for plan implementation.
  Example: Assisting communities with developing long-term recovery plans.

- Provide technical assistance such as technical advisory support, impact analyses, and Geographic Information Systems (GIS) analyses.

- Host peer-to-peer training series for SLTT partners regarding disaster recovery processes, planning, and capacity considerations.
  Example: Developing and hosting Just in Time Recovery Management Training series.

PARTICIPATING AGENCIES AND ORGANIZATIONS

American Red Cross | AmeriCorps | Delta Regional Authority | Department of Agriculture | Department of Commerce | Department of Education | Department of Justice | Department of Health and Human Services | Department of Homeland Security | Department of Housing and Urban Development | Department of the Interior | Department of Transportation | Environmental Protection Agency | General Services Administration | Small Business Administration | U.S. Access Board | U.S. Army Corps of Engineers |

ECONOMIC RECOVERY SUPPORT FUNCTION

COORDINATING AGENCY: U.S. DEPARTMENT OF COMMERCE, ECONOMIC DEVELOPMENT ADMINISTRATION

MISSION

Integrate the expertise of the federal government to help state, local, Tribal Nation, and territorial governments (SLTTs) and their partners in sustaining and rebuilding businesses, revitalizing employment, and developing economic opportunities that result in sustainable, economically resilient communities after large-scale or catastrophic incidents.

BEFORE A DISASTER

BUILDING CAPACITY

- Identify risks that may affect economic assets and infrastructure and develop strategies to strengthen local economies, such as programs that encourage economic diversification.

PARTNERSHIP DEVELOPMENT

- Create opportunities for representatives of local and state economic/workforce development organizations to meet federal experts and learn about available recovery resources and assistance programs.
  Example: Collaborating with local businesses and economic development partners, including local chambers of commerce and economic development districts, to connect them to Interagency Recovery Coordination teams.
- Support local communities in developing multi-sector partnerships that can bolster economic development projects.
- Collaborate with economic development organizations on data tools, dashboards, and guides to help them plan and effectively implement recovery and resilience strategies.

PLANNING AND PREPAREDNESS

- Encourage regional economic development districts to develop Comprehensive Economic Development Strategies (CEDS) that strengthen resilience to risks and hazards, including aligning the CEDS with FEMA-approved hazard mitigation plans.
  Example: Publishing the CEDS and Hazard Mitigation Plan Alignment Guide.
- Encourage businesses to mitigate risk and create recovery strategies that ensure continuity of operations and prevent workforce and payroll disruptions.
  Example: Providing technical assistance and step-by-step support for small business disaster preparedness and recovery planning through the Small Business Administration (SBA) local Small Business Development Centers and the online Ascent platform.

ECONOMIC RECOVERY SUPPORT FUNCTION

COORDINATING AGENCY: U.S. DEPARTMENT OF COMMERCE, ECONOMIC DEVELOPMENT ADMINISTRATION

AFTER A DISASTER

BUILDING CAPACITY

- Help identify resources to fund recovery, rebuilding, and resilience efforts, which may include support for disaster recovery coordinators and project funding.
  Example: Providing SBA "boots on the ground" to deliver disaster lending programs to homeowners, renters, nonprofits, and small businesses in the aftermath of a disaster.

- Help disaster-affected places take advantage of new economic opportunities, build a workforce for the future, and promote rebuilding efforts that add value to the local economy.
  Example: Administering the Department of Labor Dislocated Worker Program to support workers who have lost jobs due to disaster and engaging state vocational rehabilitation programs to assist individuals with disabilities in gaining or regaining employment.

- Provide financial and technical support utilizing SBA resources to help businesses stabilize in the immediate aftermath of a disaster, build back stronger, and support a foundation for long term economic and community recovery.
  Example: Leveraging district offices, Small Business Development Centers, and disaster loans and grants to repair and rebuild; providing mitigation options to build back stronger; and making small business government contracts available for disaster response and recovery efforts.

- Provide grants, technical guidance, and loans to support small business development in new and emerging sectors of local and regional economies.

TECHNICAL ASSISTANCE, TOOLS, AND TRAINING

- Provide technical assistance and economic development data analysis to local and regional leadership.
  Example: Coordinating activities with FEMA and SLTTs to deliver early economic stabilization during recovery efforts following Hurricane Helene; providing pre- and post-disaster economic analysis of impacted communities; connecting local businesses and economic development partners to provide federal technical assistance and potential funding.

- Implement workforce development initiatives that provide economically displaced survivors with vocational training for current and emerging employment opportunities, as well as short-term employment opportunities for displaced workers.

- Conduct research studies investigating workforce capacity, supply chain, and infrastructure issues that may hinder recovery, and identify ways to overcome these barriers to encourage economic diversification and growth.
  Example: Conducting Workforce and Laborshed Assessment Studies, such as the study developed in the aftermath of Hurricane Maria.

PARTICIPATING AGENCIES AND ORGANIZATIONS

AmeriCorps | Department of Agriculture | Department of Energy | Department of Health and Human Services | Department of Housing and Urban Development | Department of the Interior | Department of Labor | Department of Homeland Security | Department of the Treasury | Department of Transportation | Environmental Protection Agency | Federal Emergency Management Agency | Small Business Administration

HEALTH, EDUCATION, AND HUMAN SERVICES RECOVERY SUPPORT FUNCTION

COORDINATING AGENCY: U.S. DEPARTMENT OF HEALTH AND HUMAN SERVICES, ADMINISTRATION FOR STRATEGIC PREPAREDNESS AND RESPONSE

MISSION

Assist locally led recovery efforts to restore public health, health care, human services, education, and behavioral health networks to promote the resilience, health, and well-being of affected individuals and communities.

BEFORE A DISASTER

BUILDING CAPACITY

- Develop tools and materials and promote resources to increase the capacity of health, education, and human services providers and agencies.
  Example: Providing Positive Behavioral Interventions & Supports (PBIS), and Train the Trainer engagements related to clinical and subclinical topics.

PARTNERSHIP DEVELOPMENT

- Identify, connect, and coordinate with Health, Education, and Human Services partners at federal, state, local, Tribal Nation, and territorial governments (SLTTs), as well as non-governmental organizations, including state education agencies and the Association of State and Territorial Health Officials.

PLANNING AND PREPAREDNESS

- Promote continued learning and expansion of scientific knowledge to inform recovery from disasters and public health emergencies.
  Example: Offering training at Substance Abuse and Mental Health Services Administration (SAMHSA) Disaster Technical Assistance Centers, Centers for Disease Control and Prevention (CDC), and National Institute of Health Academies.

TECHNICAL ASSISTANCE, TOOLS, AND TRAINING

- Provide comprehensive emergency management training to community leaders, local officials, state education agencies, and institutions of higher education on both pre- and post-disaster interventions to equip them for effective disaster recovery.
  Example: Training on promoting behavioral health outcomes through techniques like Psychological First Aid and Skills for Psychological Recovery.

- Develop and distribute materials to build resilience and support preparedness planning at Technical Assistance Centers.
  Example: Distributing Readiness and Emergency Management for Schools (REMS) Technical Assistance, Administration for Strategic Prepardness and Response Technical Resources Assistance Center and Information Exchange, and SAMHSA Disaster Technical Assistance Center.

HEALTH, EDUCATION, AND HUMAN SERVICES RECOVERY SUPPORT FUNCTION

COORDINATING AGENCY: U.S. DEPARTMENT OF HEALTH AND HUMAN SERVICES, ADMINISTRATION FOR STRATEGIC PREPAREDNESS AND RESPONSE

AFTER A DISASTER

BUILDING CAPACITY

- Support the development of strategies to restore community healthcare capacity and help affected healthcare facilities strengthen emergency preparedness and readiness plans.

- Assist SLTTs with identifying specific federal resources, navigating the complexities of available funding, and identifying appropriate pathways to help address key health, education, or human services challenges.
  Example: Providing REMS Technical Assistance, PBIS Technical Assessment Center, and the Community Assessment for Public Health Emergency Response.

- Advise on relevant human services programs waivers and flexibilities such as children, families, older adults, and individuals with access and functional needs, enabling those programs to support community recovery more directly (including childcare, domestic violence services, and aging and disability networks).
  Example: Advising partners on childcare licensure and subsidy grants as well as means-tested social services programs (Supplemental Nutrition Assistance Program and Special Supplemental Nutrition Program for Women, Infants, and Children) and workforce participation programs.

- Advise affected K-12 schools and institutions of higher education on how to restore a safe environment conducive to learning, including the U.S. Department of Education's Project School Emergency Response to Violence grant and other applicable grants and regulatory flexibilities.
  Example: Directing partners to resources and guidance found at the U.S. Department of Education Natural Disaster Resources website.

PARTNERSHIP DEVELOPMENT

- Address cross cutting recovery issues for health, education, and human services related to the needs of children, youth, and families; integrate older adults and people with access and functional needs; plan for future disaster risks; and focus on rural and underserved communities.
  Example: Conducting community level behavioral health, environmental health assessments that include specific attention to youth and older adults, disability integration, and holistic restoration of health, education, and human services systems.

PLANNING AND PREPAREDNESS

- Assist SLTTs in developing and incorporating plans for the transition from post-disaster recovery operations back to steady-state operations.

HEALTH, EDUCATION, AND HUMAN SERVICES RECOVERY SUPPORT FUNCTION

COORDINATING AGENCY: U.S. DEPARTMENT OF HEALTH AND HUMAN SERVICES, ADMINISTRATION FOR STRATEGIC PREPAREDNESS AND RESPONSE

AFTER A DISASTER (CONT.)

TECHNICAL ASSISTANCE, TOOLS, AND TRAINING

- Perform needs assessments, including rapid community needs assessments such as the CDC's Community Assessment for Public Health Emergency Response, and develop courses of action to support SLTT recovery strategies, focusing on specialized technical assistance, scientific subject matter expertise, peer-to-peer support, and programmatic technical assistance.
- Facilitate discussions between state educational youth and State Coordinators for the Education of Children and Youth Experiencing Homelessness on best practices and lessons learned to support homeless and displaced students.
- Conduct after action reviews for state education agencies about their disaster recovery efforts to capture best practices, lessons learned, and recommendations for future disasters.
- Deliver training and assistance to assess and mitigate post-disaster environmental health hazards such as mold, lead, asbestos, industrial chemicals, or airborne particulate matter.
Example: Deploying mold experts to train and assist SLTT partners with mold related disaster environments.

PARTICIPATING AGENCIES AND ORGANIZATIONS

Administration for Children and Families | Administration for Community Living | Agency for Healthcare Research and Quality | Agency for Toxic Substances and Disease Registry | American Red Cross | AmeriCorps | Centers for Disease Control and Prevention | Centers for Medicare & Medicaid Services | Commissioned Corps of the U.S. Public Health Service | Department of Agriculture | Department of Education | Department of Veteran Affairs | Environmental Protection Agency | Food and Drug Administration | Health Resources and Services Administration | HHS Office of the Secretary | Indian Health Service | National Institutes of Health | National Voluntary Organizations Active in Disaster | Substance Abuse and Mental Health Services Administration

HOUSING RECOVERY SUPPORT FUNCTION

COORDINATING AGENCY: U.S. DEPARTMENT OF HOUSING AND URBAN DEVELOPMENT

MISSION

Provide housing development expertise while engaging in and facilitating collaboration among federal, state, local, and territorial partners involved in housing recovery. Support communities in developing a holistic, inclusive, and equitable recovery plan and implementation process. Assist in assessing impacts, determining key issues, analyzing damage data, and identifying resources, tools, and technical assistance to support the communities' resilient and sustainable rebuilding.

BEFORE A DISASTER

PLANNING AND PREPAREDNESS

- Support local planning, preparedness, education, training, and outreach efforts to enhance capabilities for long-term recovery.
  Example: Establishing the Pre-Disaster Housing Initiative and providing U.S. Department of Housing and Urban Development Disaster Resources.

TECHNICAL ASSISTANCE, TOOLS, AND TRAINING

- Provide training, tools, and resources on community housing development and rebuilding (including resiliency and mitigation efforts), programs available to state, local, Tribal Nation, and territorial governments (SLTTs) partners, and guidance on how to access these resources.
  Example: Offering training such as HUD 101 training, Community Development Block Grant Disaster Recovery (CDBG-DR) training, and technical assistance in utilizing existing CDBG funds to fill funding gaps.

AFTER A DISASTER

BUILDING CAPACITY

- Assist communities in identifying and coordinating resources that promote rebuilding efforts focused on resilience and affordable housing for individuals with access and functional needs (AFN) and other vulnerable populations.

- Assist communities in identifying and coordinating resources that support resilient rebuilding efforts and meet the affordability needs of vulnerable populations, including those with AFN.
  Example: Delivering information and resources efficiently to affected communities through the HUD CDBG-DR website and Disaster Recovery Resource events.

PARTNERSHIP DEVELOPMENT

- Lead and facilitate problem-solving among federal agencies and community partners to identify permanent housing solutions and address housing challenges related to providing affordable, accessible, and sustainable housing.
  Example: Convening other Recovery Support Functions to engage local community partners in discussions about rebuilding considerations with a focus on economic, health, and educational systems.

HOUSING RECOVERY SUPPORT FUNCTION

COORDINATING AGENCY: U.S. DEPARTMENT OF HOUSING AND URBAN DEVELOPMENT

AFTER A DISASTER (CONT.)

PLANNING AND PREPAREDNESS

- Develop a disaster data-driven Housing Impact Assessment to identify the effects on renters, homeowners, and marginalized or vulnerable populations. This assessment provides critical insights to inform potential recovery considerations and support SLTT recovery plans.

- Develop a data-driven Housing Impact Assessment that identifies the impacts of a disaster on renters, homeowners, marginalized communities, and vulnerable populations. This assessment provides critical insights and information to aid SLTTs in their recovery planning.
  Example: Collaborating with colleges and universities on student housing and damages data and providing comparisons between pre-disaster housing market data and impacts based on Federal Emergency Management Agency-verified losses.

TECHNICAL ASSISTANCE, TOOLS, AND TRAINING

- Provide training on housing programs available to SLTT partners and how to access the resources.
  Example: Providing resources for navigating funding sources, how to use Public Housing Agency funding effectively, how to access grant funding, and resources for understanding and accessing CDBG-DR funds, and the Rapid Unsheltered Survivor Housing Program.

PARTICIPATING AGENCIES AND ORGANIZATIONS

American Red Cross | AmeriCorps | Consumer Financial Protection Bureau | Department of Agriculture | Department of Commerce | Department of Health and Human Services | Department of Justice | Department of Veterans Affairs | Environmental Protection Agency | Federal Housing Finance Agency | Federal Emergency Management Agency | National Voluntary Organizations Active in Disaster | Small Business Administration | Department of Energy

INFRASTRUCTURE SYSTEMS RECOVERY SUPPORT FUNCTION
COORDINATING AGENCY: U.S. DEPARTMENT OF DEFENSE, U.S. ARMY CORPS OF ENGINEERS

MISSION

Provide support to state, local, Tribal Nation, and territorial governments (SLTTs) undertaking the rehabilitation and reconstruction of affected infrastructure systems through coordinated delivery of federal resources, while supporting long-term infrastructure resilience that highlights the use of new, accessible, and permanent infrastructure system options.

BEFORE A DISASTER

BUILDING CAPACITY

- Address repetitive flooding problems through floodplain management studies that develop hydraulic models, flood inundation maps, and potential flooding solutions to help affected communities.
  Example: Managing U.S. Army Corps of Engineers (USACE) programs to reduce flood risk including Continuing Authorities Program (CAP) Section 205 Flood Risk Reduction Projects, Planning Assistance to States (PAS) studies, Floodplain Management Services (FPMS) projects, and Silver Jackets projects.

PARTNERSHIP DEVELOPMENT

- Conduct Resilience Improvement Plan webinars that highlight benefits and necessary steps for highway and roadway resilience improvements.
  Example: Providing roadway protection through CAP Section 205 Flood Risk Reduction Projects and CAP Section 14 Emergency Bank Stabilization.

PLANNING AND PREPAREDNESS

- Plan federal support for disaster recovery, ranging from catastrophic incidents to regional disaster recovery challenges.
  Example: Supporting emergency management planning through PL-84-99 authorities, managing Hurricane Evacuation Studies for most states, and supporting planning through Silver Jackets activities, PAS studies, and FPMS projects.

TECHNICAL ASSISTANCE, TOOLS, AND TRAINING

- Provide SLTTs with hazard mitigation technical assistance.
  Example: Assisting through PAS, Silver Jackets, and FPMS projects.

- Deliver evacuation modeling technical assistance that addresses specific disaster types.
  Example: Conducting hurricane evacuation studies for coastal states, and modelling evacuations in collaboration with the Institute for Water Resources.

INFRASTRUCTURE SYSTEMS RECOVERY SUPPORT FUNCTION

COORDINATING AGENCY: U.S. DEPARTMENT OF DEFENSE, U.S. ARMY CORPS OF ENGINEERS

AFTER A DISASTER

PLANNING AND PREPAREDNESS

- Promote resiliency strategies that consider and respect cultural and community concerns. Example: Providing technical assistance through programs like Silver Jackets, FPMS, PAS, and USACE Centers of Expertise to ensure resilience measures align with community values and traditions.

TECHNICAL ASSISTANCE, TOOLS, AND TRAINING

- Provide technical assistance to develop recovery strategies, such as a Wildfire Watershed Recovery Strategy. Example: Providing CAP Section 205 Flood Risk Reduction Projects, CAP Section 206 Aquatic Resource Restoration, PAS studies, FPMS projects, Silver Jackets projects, and watershed studies under Section 729 of the Water Resources Development Act of 1986.

- Assist SLTTs with conducting detailed analysis, developing response strategies, and identifying resource needs. Example: Providing technical assistance through programs like Silver Jackets, FPMS, PAS, and USACE Centers of Expertise.

PARTICIPATING AGENCIES AND ORGANIZATIONS

Cybersecurity and Infrastructure Security Agency | Delta Regional Authority | Department of Agriculture | Department of Commerce | Department of Defense | Department of Energy | Department of Homeland Security | Department of Housing and Urban Development | Department of the Interior | Department of Transportation | Environmental Protection Agency | Federal Communications Commission | Federal Emergency Management Agency | General Services Administration | Nuclear Regulatory Commission | Tennessee Valley Authority | U.S. Fire Administration | Department of the Treasury

NATURAL AND CULTURAL RESOURCES RECOVERY SUPPORT FUNCTION

COORDINATING AGENCY: U.S. DEPARTMENT OF THE INTERIOR

MISSION

Assist state, local, Tribal Nation, and territorial governments (SLTTs) in the protection, preservation, and recovery of natural and cultural resources after disaster. Natural resources are land, fish, wildlife, biota, air, and water. Cultural resources are tangible entities or cultural practices that represent the diverse history, art, and traditions of our nation.

BEFORE A DISASTER

BUILDING CAPACITY

- Support the establishment of traditional trades apprenticeship programs to address the shortage of skilled artisans and professionals trained to protect, conserve, and restore cultural resources.
Example: Coordinating with nonprofit organizations to augment staff and provide conservation support, as provided through the National Park Service for the San Juan National Historic Site alongside the American Conservation Experience.

- Support the creation of targeted guidance and tools for SLTTs involved in the protection of natural and cultural resources.
Example: Creating historic preservation guides for states and Tribal Nations on working with the federal government before and after disasters.

PLANNING AND PREPAREDNESS

- In collaboration with SLTT partners, identify gaps and inconsistencies among relevant regulations, policies, program requirements, and processes used in disaster recovery that affect natural and cultural resources. Upon identification, offer recommendations to Federal Emergency Management Agency (FEMA) and other federal agencies.
Example: Identifying a lack of Tribal Nation engagement and the need for additional consultation with partners not immediately identified after the disaster, and in another instance, the identification of invasive species concerns within redevelopment plans.

AFTER A DISASTER

PARTNERSHIP DEVELOPMENT

- Provide public outreach, studies, plans, and financial assistance to help communities with rebuilding and reimagining local recreational opportunities.

  Example: Supporting development activities for Recovery Master Plans, as provided for the Blue River Park Wildfire Recovery Master Plan by the National Park Service Rivers, Trails, and Conservation Assistance Program and funded by FEMA.

NATURAL AND CULTURAL RESOURCES RECOVERY SUPPORT FUNCTION

COORDINATING AGENCY: U.S. DEPARTMENT OF THE INTERIOR

AFTER A DISASTER (CONT.)

PARTNERSHIP DEVELOPMENT

- Facilitate meetings with Tribal government officials and intergovernmental partners to identify unmet needs and introduce steady-state federal and nonprofit resources that can be leveraged to address recovery challenges.
Example: Establishing working relationships through Memorandums of Understanding with Tribal Nation leadership and federal agencies, as coordinated during recovery efforts after the Las Conchas Fire in 2011 and subsequent flooding in 2013.

- Communicate the importance of natural and cultural resource recovery at meetings, webinars, and conferences.
Example: Providing information sessions highlighting the work of the Natural and Cultural Resources Recovery Support Function and the ways it has assisted the preservation of collections, art, archives, buildings, and other cultural assets.

PLANNING AND PREPAREDNESS

- Promote SLTT consideration of natural and cultural resources as part of recovery planning, priorities, and goals.
Example: Incorporating actions in Recovery Support Strategies to promote the protection, rehabilitation, and restoration of natural and cultural resources.

- Integrate sustainable planning elements that consider long-term environmental effects to natural resources, including open spaces, recreational areas, and ecologically sensitive resources.
Example: Working with local universities through the National Oceanic and Atmospheric Administration National Sea Grant College program to facilitate research on nature-based solutions to mitigate coastal erosion. Nature-based solutions involve intentionally using natural and nature-based features, like beaches, dunes, islands, marshes and mangroves, and coral and oyster reefs to absorb and protect shorelines during storm events.

TECHNICAL ASSISTANCE, TOOLS, AND TRAINING

- Promote sharing and integration of natural and cultural resource impact data among SLTTs.
Example: Providing access to tools and informational products through the U.S. Geological Survey (USGS) for storm events, the USGS Streamgage Network, USGS Flood Event Viewer, and other data and mapping resources for disaster events.

- Assist SLTT partners with identifying federal, nonprofit, and philanthropic partners to leverage SLTT investments in recovery.
Example: Providing workshops for funding and technical assistance through the National Endowment for the Arts, National Endowment for the Humanities, and the Institute of Museum and Library Services.

PARTICIPATING AGENCIES AND ORGANIZATIONS

Advisory Council on Historic Preservation | AmeriCorps | Council on Environmental Quality | Cybersecurity and Infrastructure Security Agency | Department of Agriculture | Department of Commerce | Department of Education | Environmental Protection Agency | Federal Emergency Management Agency | General Services Administration | Heritage Emergency National Task Force | U.S. Army Corps of Engineers

Appendix B: Acronyms

Table 1: Acronyms

Acronym	Definition
AFN	Access and Functional Needs
ASPR	Administration for Strategic Preparedness and Response
CDBG-DR	Community Development Block Grant Disaster Recovery
CAP	Continuing Authorities Program
CDC	Centers for Disease Control and Prevention
CEDS	Comprehensive Economic Development Strategies
CFRC	Chief Federal Response Coordinator
DHS	U.S. Department of Homeland Security
DOC	U.S. Department of Commerce
DOI	U.S. Department of the Interior
EDA	Economic Development Administration
EPA	Environmental Protection Agency
FCO	Federal Coordinating Officer
FDRC	Federal Disaster Recovery Coordinator
FDRO	Federal Disaster Recovery Officer
FEMA	Federal Emergency Management Agency
FIOP	Federal Interagency Operational Plan
FPMS	Floodplain Management Services
GIS	Geographic Information System
HHS	U.S. Department of Health and Human Services
HMGP	Hazard Mitigation Grant Program
HUD	U.S. Department of Housing and Urban Development
IAA	Interagency Agreements
IRC	Interagency Recovery Coordination
IRWA	Interagency Reimbursable Work Agreements
JFO	Joint Field Office

Acronym	Definition
LDRM	Local Disaster Recovery Manager
LTRG	Long-Term Recovery Group
MOU	Memorandum of Understanding
NDRF	National Disaster Recovery Framework
NGO	Nongovernmental Organization
NOAA	National Oceanic and Atmospheric Administration
NPG	National Preparedness Goal
NRF	National Response Framework
PAS	Planning Assistance to States
PBIS	Positive Behavioral Interventions & Supports
PDHI	Pre-Disaster Housing Initiative
REMS	Readiness and Emergency Management for Schools
RSF	Recovery Support Function
SAMHSA	Substance Abuse and Mental Health Services Administration
SBA	Small Business Administration
SBDC	Small Business Development Center
SDRC	State Disaster Recovery Coordinator
SLTT	State, Local, Tribal Nation, and Territorial governments
SPR	State Preparedness Report
TDRC	Territory Disaster Recovery Coordinator
Tribal DRC	Tribal Disaster Recovery Coordinator
THIRA	Threat and Hazard Identification and Risk Assessment
USACE	U.S. Army Corps of Engineers
VAL	Volunteer Agency Liaison
VOAD	Voluntary Organizations Active in Disaster

Appendix C: Glossary

Access and Functional Needs (AFN) – Persons who may have additional needs before, during, and after an incident in functional areas, including but not limited to maintaining independence, communication, transportation, supervision, and medical care. Individuals in need of additional assistance may include those who have disabilities, live in institutionalized settings, are seniors, are children, are from diverse cultures, have limited English proficiency or are non-English speaking, or lack access to reliable transportation.

Accessibility – The design, construction, development, and maintenance of facilities, information and communication technology, programs, and services so that all people, including people with disabilities, can fully and independently use them. Accessibility includes the provision of accommodations and modifications to ensure equal access to employment and participation in activities for people with disabilities, the reduction or elimination of physical and attitudinal barriers to equitable opportunities, a commitment to ensuring that people with disabilities can independently access every outward-facing and internal activity or electronic space, and the pursuit of best practices such as universal design.

Advisor – High-level subject-matter specialists assigned to support a recovery mission with extensive knowledge of how their department or agency's programs operate. Their expertise is brought in to supplement the Recovery Support Function (RSF) Field Coordinators as needed. Advisors can support the Federal Disaster Recovery Officer (FDRO) and Field Coordinators in developing an approach to support a recovery mission unique to the local communities and/or region. Advisors also help Recovery's leadership and staff understand their agencies' authorities and senior leadership functions at the incident level.

Community Foundations – Grantmaking public charities that focus on improving the lives of people in a specific geographic area. They bring together financial resources from individuals, families, and businesses to support effective nonprofits in their communities.

Community Lifelines – Services that are essential to human health and safety or economic security and enable the continuous operation of critical government and business functions.

Disability – Under the Rehabilitation Act of 1973, a physical or mental impairment that substantially limits one or more major life activities. People with disabilities give the disability inclusion mission its primary focus, with certain access and functional needs (AFN) as an extension of that focus.

Disaster Any catastrophic incident that occurs in any part of the United States, which causes damage of sufficient severity and magnitude to warrant the provision of major disaster assistance by the federal government to supplement the efforts and available resources of state, local, Tribal Nation, and territorial government (SLTT) governments and disaster relief organizations in alleviating the damage, loss, hardship, or suffering caused thereby. Catastrophic incidents can include any natural catastrophe (including any hurricane, tornado, storm, high water, wind-driven water, tidal wave, tsunami, earthquake, volcanic eruption, landslide, mudslide, snowstorm, or drought), as well as technological accidents and human-caused events, or, regardless of cause, any fire, flood, or explosion.

Equity – As defined by FEMA, the consistent and systematic fair, just, and impartial treatment of all individuals, including individuals who belong to underserved communities of color, persons who belong to communities that may face discrimination based on sex, sexual orientation, and gender identity (including members of the Lesbian, Gay, Bisexual, Transgender, and Queer + [LGBTQ+] community), persons with disabilities, persons who may face discrimination based on their religion and/or national origin, persons with limited English proficiency, and persons who live in rural areas that have been systematically denied a full opportunity to participate in aspects of economic, social, and civic life.

Federal Coordinating Officer (FCO) – The FCO is appointed by the FEMA Administrator on behalf of the president to coordinate federal assistance following a declared disaster or emergency. The FCO establishes the Joint Field Office (JFO) and works in partnership with the state, local, Tribal Nation, and territorial government (SLTT) partners to determine state and local disaster assistance requirements. For all Stafford Act-declared incidents, the FCO reports to the Regional Administrator for the region in which the incident occurs. The FCO establishes an organization to best partner with SLTT partners to achieve recovery outcomes and is responsible for the overall management of the federal response to the incident.

Federal Disaster Recovery Coordinator (FDRC) – In large-scale disasters and catastrophic incidents where a federal role may be necessary, the FDRC has the role of incorporating recovery and mitigation considerations into the early decision-making processes. The FDRC monitors the impacts and results of such decisions and evaluates the need for additional assistance and adjustments where necessary and feasible throughout the disaster recovery. The FDRC is responsible for facilitating disaster recovery coordination and collaboration between the Federal, Tribal Nation, and state and local governments, business and industry, and voluntary, faith-based and community organizations. The FDRC partners with and supports the Local Disaster Recovery Manager (LDRM) and the State, Territorial, and/or Tribal Disaster Recovery Coordinator (SDRC, TDRC, and/or Tribal DRC) to facilitate disaster recovery in the affected State or Tribal area.

Federal Disaster Recovery Officer (FDRO) – The FDRO is appointed by the Federal Coordinator Officer (FCO) when an enhanced level of Interagency Recovery Coordination (IRC) is needed. When appointed, the FDRO serves as the primary advisor to the FCO or Federal Disaster Recovery Coordinator (FDRC) on all recovery issues.

Hazard – A source or cause of harm or difficulty.

Interagency Reimbursable Work Agreement (IRWA) – An agreement between federal agencies where one agency obtains supplies or services from another federal agency and that agency provides the supplies and services using its own resources (e.g., employees, contracts, inventory). IRWAs are executed under the authority of the DHS Chief Financial Officer (CFO). For DHS policy on IRWAs see Department of Homeland Security Acquisition Manual Chapter 3, Section 3.7, Intergovernmental Actions, Transactions, and Reporting of the DHS CFO Financial Management Policy Manual. Examples of IRWAs are reimbursement for salaries of temporarily detailed employees and Reimbursable Work Authorizations for building renovations requested through the General Services Administration such as those entered under the authority of 40 U.S.C. 592(b)(2).

Interagency Agreement (IAA) – A written agreement between federal agencies (or Components within a federal agency), which is part of an inter- or intra-agency transaction, for supplies and services to be provided by a servicing agency in support of a requesting agency. An IAA is required for assisted acquisitions and Interagency Reimbursable Work Agreements (IRWAs). Specific formats of IAAs are negotiated between agencies, also known as Trading Partners.

Joint Field Office (JFO) – The unified command center of the disaster. FEMA, state or Tribal Administration staff, and other federal agencies are primarily located in the JFO. It is also the location of the Federal Coordinating Officer (FCO). Unlike the Disaster Recovery Center, it is not a physical location for directly servicing disaster survivors. The JFO is a management office and provides services remotely. The JFO's physical location varies depending on the disaster. It is often in the state capital or located near or adjacent to disaster-affected areas. The JFOs are dependent on the size and scope of the disaster, as well as on available amenities such as electricity, water, and lodging.

Local Disaster Recovery Manager (LDRM) – Serves as the central manager to organize, coordinate, and advance recovery for the jurisdiction, facilitating an effective and efficient local recovery. This position may be appointed for disaster recovery, or permanently staffed to coordinate recovery activities through pre-disaster recovery planning and post-disaster recovery plan, partnership engagement, operational coordination, and resource identification. LDRMs may serve as the jurisdiction's primary point of contact with both government and nongovernment agencies and collaborate across partners to coordinate sustained financial support for recovery.

Long-Term Recovery Group (LTRG) - LTRGs are independent of FEMA or any other federal agency and consist of a coalition of organizations ranging from the national to the neighborhood level. Their role is to help meet the remaining needs of survivors after they have maximized state and federal funds available to them. LTRGs typically include federal partners, voluntary agencies, and grassroots organizations. These partnerships require close coordination to address community needs, distribute resources and to help restore vital support systems – health, social, economic, and environmental systems, among others.

Mission Assignment - A work order issued by FEMA to another Federal agency in anticipation of, or in response to, a presidential declaration of an emergency or major disaster, authorized by the Stafford Act. Mission assignments allow for deployment, employment, and assistance from the full range of federal resources to support disaster needs.

Mitigation – Capabilities necessary to reduce loss of life and property by lessening the impact of disasters. Mitigation capabilities include but are not limited to community-wide risk reduction projects, efforts to improve the resilience of critical infrastructure and key resource lifelines, risk reduction for specific vulnerabilities from natural hazards or acts of terrorism, and initiatives to reduce future risks after a disaster has occurred.

National Coordinator – Each Recovery Support Function (RSF) Coordinating Agency designates a senior staff member to serve as the RSF National Coordinator. The RSF National Coordinator provides significant engagement and management for the RSF and encourages ongoing communication and coordination between the RSF agencies to ensure successful mission delivery.

Nongovernmental Organization – NGOs include Voluntary Organizations Active in Disaster (VOAD) and other nonprofits, encompassing voluntary, faith- and community-based, business and industry, philanthropic, minority or disability-focused groups, and whole community partners who help individuals and communities equitably plan for, respond to, and recover from disasters.

Planning – The deliberate process of determining how (the ways) to coordinate and use a partner's capabilities (the means) in time and space to achieve objectives (the ends) while addressing the associated risks.

Preparedness – Actions that involve a combination of planning, resources, training, exercising, and organizing to build, sustain, and improve operational capabilities. Preparedness is the process of identifying the personnel, training, and equipment needed for a wide range of potential incidents and developing jurisdiction-specific plans for delivering capabilities when needed for an incident.

Prevention – Capabilities necessary to avoid, prevent, or stop a threatened or actual act of terrorism. Prevention capabilities include, but are not limited to, information sharing and warning, domestic counterterrorism, and preventing the acquisition or use of weapons of mass destruction. For purposes of the prevention framework called for in Presidential Policy Directive 8, the term "prevention" refers to preventing imminent threats.

Protection - Actions to protect citizens, residents, visitors, and assets against the greatest threats and hazards in a manner that allows American interests, aspirations, and way of life to thrive.

Recovery – The timely restoration, strengthening and revitalization of infrastructure, housing, and a sustainable economy, as well as the health, social, cultural, historic, and environmental fabric of communities affected by an incident.

Recovery Needs Assessment – A systematic evaluation to identify and prioritize the needs of a community following a disaster, including damage assessment, resource gaps, and immediate and long-term recovery requirements.

Recovery Support Function (RSF) Coordinating Agency – The main Coordinating Agency responsible for managing the RSF and its participating agencies and organizations. Each RSF Coordinating Agency designates a senior-level principal to serve as the RSF National Coordinator, provides significant engagement and management for the RSF, and encourages ongoing communication and coordination between the Coordinating Agency and participating agencies and organizations and between state or other federal RSFs.

Recovery Support Function (RSF) Field Coordinator – For each RSF activated, an RSF Field Coordinator is designated to serve as the federal point person for coordination at the field level. Each RSF Field Coordinator has specific subject-matter expertise and is mission assigned to the incident in coordination with the National Coordinator, Federal Disaster Recovery Coordinator (FDRC), Federal Disaster Recovery Officer (FDRO), and other RSFs involved in the recovery operation.

Recovery Support Function (RSF) Participating Agency/Organization – Each RSF is comprised of multiple federal agencies that have a role to play in that RSF's mission, known as participating agencies and organizations. The RSF National Coordinator will work with their RSF participating agencies and organizations as needed to address the specific needs of a community following an incident. Participating agencies and organizations may not be necessary for every incident.

Recovery Support Strategy – A comprehensive report developed by Interagency Recovery Coordination (IRC) to align federal resources, such as funding and technical assistance, with the recovery needs and priorities identified by SLTT partners. Serving as a strategic roadmap, this document fosters a holistic understanding of recovery support activities and promotes a coordinated approach to delivering federal and SLTT recovery assistance.

Resilience – The ability to prepare for threats and hazards, adapt to changing conditions, and withstand and recover rapidly from adverse conditions and disruptions.

Response – Capabilities necessary to save lives, protect property and the environment, and meet basic human needs after an incident has occurred.

Restoration – Returning a physical structure, essential government or commercial services, or a societal condition back to a former or normal state of use through repairs, rebuilding, or re-establishment.

Risk – The potential for an unwanted outcome resulting from an incident, event, or occurrence, as determined by its likelihood and the associated consequences. Continuity plans and programs mitigate risk from threats and hazards to the performance of essential functions and associated critical infrastructure.

State Disaster Recovery Coordinator (SDRC) – This position may be appointed for disaster recovery, or permanently staffed to organize, coordinate, and advance the recovery at the state level. The SDRC works closely with local officials, particularly Local Disaster Recovery Managers (LDRMs), to help communicate local recovery priorities and resources to federal officials. The SDRC establishes or leads a state-wide structure for managing the recovery. The SDRC is the link between local recovery operations and the resources available at the state and federal levels. The SDRC is responsible for facilitating communication between federal and local efforts while also coordinating with other state agencies.

Steady State – A state where operations and procedures are normal and ongoing. Communities are considered to be at a steady state and undergo steady state activities prior to disasters and after recovery is complete.

Sustainability – Meeting the needs of the present without compromising the ability of future generations to meet their own needs.

Territorial Disaster Recovery Coordinator (TDRC) – The role tasked to organize, coordinate, and advance the recovery at the territorial level. The TDRC works closely with local officials to help communicate local recovery priorities and resources to federal officials. The TDRC establishes or leads a territory-wide structure for managing the recovery and serves as the link between local recovery operations and the resources available at the state and federal levels. The TDRC is responsible for facilitating communication between federal and local efforts while also coordinating with other territorial agencies.

Threat – Include capabilities, intentions, and attack methods of adversaries used to exploit circumstances or occurrences with the intent to cause harm.

Tribal Disaster Recovery Coordinator (Tribal DRC) – The Tribal DRC works closely with federal and sometimes state and local officials to communicate Tribal recovery priorities. The role can be staffed to organize, coordinate, and advance the recovery at the Tribal level. The Tribal DRC establishes or leads a Tribal structure for managing recovery. The Tribal DRC has responsibilities that are similar to a Local Disaster Recovery Manager (LDRM) and State Disaster Recovery Coordinator (SDRC). The Tribal DRC's responsibilities may overlap those of an LDRM, if an LDRM is not designated for a particular district or locality.

Voluntary Agency Liaison (VAL) – FEMA Voluntary Agency Liaisons (VALs) establish, foster, and maintain relationships among government, voluntary, faith, and community-based, private sector, and philanthropic partners. Through these relationships, the VALs support the delivery of services and empower and equip communities to address disaster-caused unmet needs.

Voluntary Organizations Active in Disasters (VOADs) – A coalition of nonprofit organizations that collaborate to provide assistance and support during all phases of disaster response and recovery. VOADs operate at national, state, and local levels to coordinate efforts, maximize resources, and ensure effective service delivery to affected communities.

Vulnerable Populations – Populations that are less likely to be able to prepare for hazards; less likely to receive or be able to respond to warnings; more likely to die, suffer injuries, and have disproportionately higher material losses; have more psychological trauma; and face more obstacles during phases of response and recovery. While vulnerable populations can be located in any area, all people located in a geographically isolated location are considered vulnerable populations. While vulnerable populations can be located in any area, all people located in a geographically isolated location are considered vulnerable populations.

Whole Community – A focus on enabling the participation in national preparedness activities of a wider range of players from the private and nonprofit sectors, including nongovernmental organizations and the public, in conjunction with the participation of all levels of government to foster better coordination and working relationships. Used interchangeably with "all-of-Nation."

National Disaster Recovery Framework – Third Edition

Appendix D: Pre-disaster Recovery Planning and Post-disaster Recovery Planning

This appendix includes examples of pre- and post-disaster recovery planning activities, as well as examples of how to use data to measure progress.

Table 2: Pre-disaster Recovery Planning

Planning Activities	Examples
Organizational Framework	- Establish clear leadership, coordination, and decision-making throughout all levels of government. - Identify a Local Disaster Recovery Manager, or the State, Territory, or Tribal Disaster Recovery Coordinator as appropriate.
Identify existing capability and capacity	- Identify hazards and assess risks and vulnerabilities to include place-based resilience and mitigation issues.[18] - Identify limitations in recovery capacity. - Evaluate the likely conditions and needs after a disaster.
Assess gaps and requirements	- Develop initial situational awareness. - Identify goals and priorities for the communities. - Assess gaps and requirements (e.g., policies, resources, training, operations, systems, data) to meet those goals. - Integrate with other appropriate community planning (e.g., accessibility design, capital improvement planning).
Identify Roles and Responsibilities	- Identify how the community will work together after a disaster to develop their plan for recovery. - Identify sectors of the community to participate in pre- and post-disaster recovery planning and coordination. - Prepare pre-disaster Memorandum of Understanding to establish early partnerships, and expectations with community faith-based organizations, nonprofit groups, and business and industry partners.
Partnership Engagement	- Develop a communication plan that includes and considers indigenous languages. - Identify and engage the public, community leaders, faith-based organizations, nonprofit organizations, and business and industry throughout the process. - Ensure community participation of historically underserved populations including diverse racial and ethnic communities, individuals with disabilities and others with access and functional needs, children, seniors, and individuals with limited English proficiency.
Capacity Building	- Test and evaluate pre-disaster recovery plans through seminars, workshops, and exercises. - Build partnerships between neighborhoods and local government agencies that form the basis for pre-and post-multi hazard assessments and support for mitigation actions. - Develop and implement recovery training and education as a tool for building recovery capacity and making it available to all other partners.
Concept of Operations	- Establish the operational framework that is followed immediately after a disaster occurs. - Establish maintenance procedures for updating pre- and post-disaster recovery plans.
Continuous Improvement	- Identify priority recovery and redevelopment activities. - Set recovery goals and objectives. - Measure progress against those goals and objectives. - Evaluate performance and revise pre-disaster recovery plans accordingly.

---

[18] Includes wild/rural/urban interfaces, floodplain management, coastal zones, seismic areas, historic and cultural properties, districts, landscapes, and traditional cultural properties.

Table 3: Post-disaster Recovery Planning

Planning Activities	Examples
Organizational Framework	<ul><li>Identify an individual or group as well as supporting structures required to lead the process.</li><li>Coordinate with all community leaders to ensure participation and validity of the process.</li><li>Identify outside resources, financial and technical, that provide support to the overall recovery effort.</li></ul>
Needs Assessment	<ul><li>Leverage existing recovery plans and mitigation plans as foundational documents.</li><li>Assess the need created by the disaster to determine where recovery issues are present (e.g., community, economy, housing, health, education, social, infrastructure, natural, cultural).</li><li>Determine areas of focus for building future resilience through mitigation and adaptation opportunities and the impact these areas have on recovery.</li><li>Identify areas that strengthen and revitalize the community, and areas of opportunity in recovery planning.</li></ul>
Partnership Engagement	<ul><li>Solicit public participation in the development and confirmation of the vision and goals. Establish an accessible process for exchanging information between the public and leadership.</li><li>Develop a communications map to ensure all sectors of the community are engaged in the process, to include using non-traditional communications outlets to reach as much of the community as possible.</li><li>Ensure effective communications for all participants, including individuals with disabilities and individuals with limited English proficiency.</li><li>Emphasize transparent and open communication by providing drafts to partners and community members, with a recognition that plans will need be iterative.</li></ul>
Develop and document the recovery vision and goals	<ul><li>Document the vision, goals, projects, and programs.</li><li>Develop projects and programs – to include schedules and milestones to meet the recovery vision and goals created by the community.</li><li>Identify key leaders responsible for undertaking next steps or moving recovery strategies forward and determine the implementation plan and priorities for recovery projects.</li><li>Use existing public and private resources and new funding streams to creatively package resources. For example, projects can be phased for flexible application of funding.</li><li>Evaluate projects and programs to determine their impact on recovery, feasibility, public support, sustainability initiatives, effective use of resources and other criteria as determined by the community.</li></ul>
Continuous Improvement	<ul><li>Revise plans as needed to meet changing recovery needs and priorities.</li><li>Continue to update and engage the broader partner population on next steps.</li><li>Monitor progress and convey achievements to all partners.</li></ul>

Table 4: Strategies for Measuring Progress Through Data

Strategies for Measuring Progress	Examples
Technology and Systems	- Identify and access data to inform pre-disaster recovery planning from appropriate federal, state, local, and nongovernmental sources, such as those managed by the National Oceanic and Atmospheric Administration, U.S. Census Bureau, and/or state emergency management agencies. - Identify community engagement tools to solicit feedback from community and recovery partners, such as SurveyMonkey, to conduct needs assessments and measure satisfaction with recovery efforts. - Identify and establish systems that track pre-disaster baseline conditions, including Geographic Information System (GIS) tools like Environmental Systems Research Institute's Aeronautical Reconnaissance Coverage GIS and/or Quantum GIS. - Leverage technology and systems innovations to achieve goals that result in greater information sharing, accountability, and transparency.
Key Indicators	- Ensure full community participation[19] in developing metrics in coordination with partners. - Establish indicators to recovery priorities and resource needs and set realistic expectations and milestones for community members, partners, and participating agencies and organizations.
Continuous Improvement	- Ensure continuous improvement by evaluating the effectiveness of recovery activities and associated metrics. - Encourage government agencies and private organizations that provide assistance to have a system of tracking their coordination and assistance efforts, ensuring accountability, and enabling prompt adjustments to meet ongoing and changing needs.

---

[19] Includes persons with disabilities and others with access and functional needs, individuals with limited English proficiency, seniors, members of underserved populations and advocates representing the unique needs of children.

Appendix E: Digital Resource Links GENERAL RESOURCE LINKS:

- Building Private Public Partnerships Guide: https://www.fema.gov/sites/default/files/documents/fema_building-private-public-partnerships.pdf
- Climate Risk and Resilience Portal: https://climrr.anl.gov/
- Climate Adaption Planning Guide: https://www.fema.gov/sites/default/files/documents/fema_climate-adaptation-planning-guide_2024.pdf
- Community Lifelines Implementation Toolkit: https://www.fema.gov/emergency-managers/practitioners/lifelines-toolkit
- Community Recovery Management Toolkit: https://www.fema.gov/emergency-managers/national-preparedness/frameworks/community-recovery-management-toolkit
- Department of Homeland Security Acquisition Manual: https://www.dhs.gov/homeland-security-acquisition-manual
- Developing and Maintaining Emergency Operations Plans: Comprehensive Preparedness Guide 101 (CPG 101): https://www.fema.gov/sites/default/files/documents/fema_cpg-101-v3-developing-maintaining-eops.pdf
- Disaster Financial Management Guide: https://www.fema.gov/sites/default/files/2020-07/disaster-financial-management-guide.pdf
- Disaster Resource Identification Fact Sheet: https://www.fema.gov/sites/default/files/documents/fema_disaster_resource_identification_fact-sheet.pdf
- Effective Coordination of Recovery Resources for State, Tribal, Territorial, and Local Incidents: https://www.fema.gov/sites/default/files/2020-07/fema_effective-coordination-recovery-resources-guide_020515.pdf
- Engaging Faith-based and Community Organizations: https://www.fema.gov/sites/default/files/documents/fema_engaging-faith-based-and-community-organizations-guide_2024.pdf
- FEMA Case Study Library: https://www.fema.gov/emergency-managers/practitioners/case-study-library
- FEMA Emergency Management Institute (EMI): https://training.fema.gov/emi.aspx
- FEMA Post-disaster Building Safety Evaluation Guidance: https://www.fema.gov/sites/default/files/2020-07/fema_p-2055_post-disaster_buildingsafety_evaluation_2019.pdf
- FEMA Grants: https://www.fema.gov/grants
- FEMA Hazard Mitigation Planning: https://www.fema.gov/emergency-managers/risk-management/hazard-mitigation-planning
- FEMA Individual Assistance Program Policy, Guidance, and Fact Sheets: https://www.fema.gov/assistance/individual/policy-guidance-and-fact-sheets

- FEMA Public Assistance Program Policy, Guidance, and Fact Sheets: https://www.fema.gov/assistance/public/policy-guidance-fact-sheets
- FEMA Recovery and Resilience Resource Library: https://www.fema.gov/emergency-managers/practitioners/recovery-resilience-resource-library
- FEMA Risk Management: https://www.fema.gov/emergency-managers/risk-management
- Fire Management Assistance Grant Program and Policy Guide: https://www.fema.gov/assistance/public/library
- Homeland Security Information Network (HSIN): https://www.dhs.gov/homeland-security-information-network-hsin
- How a Disaster Gets Declared: https://www.fema.gov/disaster/how-declared
- Information Sharing Guide for Private-Public Partnerships: https://www.fema.gov/sites/default/files/documents/fema_information-sharing_guide.pdf
- National Building Code Adoption Tracking Portal: National Building Code Adoption Tracking Portal
- National Incident Management System: https://www.fema.gov/sites/default/files/2020-07/fema_nims_doctrine-2017.pdf
- National Incident Management System resources: https://www.fema.gov/emergency-managers/nims
- National Oceanic and Atmospheric Administration (NOAA) Digital Coast: https://coast.noaa.gov/digitalcoast
- New Recipients of Disaster Grants Guide: https://www.fema.gov/sites/default/files/2020-04/new-recipients-of-disaster-grants-guide_2019.pdf
- Non-Stafford Act Recovery Guide: Developing and Coordinating Resources, FEMA Region V: https://www.hsdl.org/?abstract&did=734289
- Planning Considerations: Disaster Housing: https://www.fema.gov/sites/default/files/2020-07/planning-considerations-disaster-housing.pdf
- Pre-Disaster Housing Planning Guide: https://www.fema.gov/sites/default/files/documents/fema_pdhi-guide.pdf
- Ready.gov: https://www.ready.gov/
- Recovery Resource Roadmap: https://www.fema.gov/emergency-managers/practitioners/roadmap-resource-library-form
- Response and Recovery Climate Change Planning Guidance: https://www.fema.gov/sites/default/files/documents/fema_response-recovery_climate-change-planning-guidance_20230630.pdf
- Restoration and Recovery Guide for Private-Public Partnerships: https://www.fema.gov/sites/default/files/documents/fema_restoration-and-recovery_guide.pdf
- Threat and Hazard Identification and Risk Assessment (THIRA) and Stakeholder Preparedness Review (SPR) Guide: CPG 201: https://www.fema.gov/sites/default/files/2020-07/threat-hazard-identification-risk-assessment-stakeholder-preparedness-review-guide.pdf
- Unified Federal Environmental and Historic Preservation Review Resources: https://www.fema.gov/emergency-managers/practitioners/environmental-historic/review
- United States (U.S.) Climate Resilience Toolkit: https://toolkit.climate.gov/

- U.S. Department of Health and Human Services Administration for Strategic Preparedness and Response: https://aspr.hhs.gov/Pages/Home.aspx
- U.S. Department of Transportation National Response and Recovery Program: https://www.transportation.gov/emergency

FEDERAL RESOURCE LINKS:

- Building Codes Adoption Playbook: https://www.fema.gov/sites/default/files/documents/fema_building-codes-adoption-playbook-for-authorities-having-jurisdiction.pdf
- Community Assistance RSF Overview: https://www.fema.gov/emergency-managers/national-preparedness/frameworks/recovery/recovery-support-functions/community-assistance-rsf
- Economic Recovery Support Function Overview: https://www.fema.gov/emergency-managers/national-preparedness/frameworks/recovery/recovery-support-functions/economic-rsf
- Federal Interagency Operational Plans: https://www.fema.gov/emergency-managers/national-preparedness/frameworks/federal-interagency-operational-plans
- FEMA Operational Planning Manual: https://emilms.fema.gov/is_2002/media/142.pdf
- FEMA Planning Guides: https://www.fema.gov/emergency-managers/national-preparedness/plan
- Health and Social Services RSF Overview: https://www.fema.gov/emergency-managers/national-preparedness/frameworks/recovery/recovery-support-functions/health-social-services-rsf
- Housing RSF Overview: https://www.fema.gov/emergency-managers/national-preparedness/frameworks/recovery/recovery-support-functions/housing-rsf
- Infrastructure RSF Overview: https://www.fema.gov/emergency-managers/national-preparedness/frameworks/recovery/recovery-support-functions/infrastructure-systems-rsf
- Long-Term Recovery Guide, National Voluntary Organizations Active in Disaster (VOAD): www.nvoad.org/wp-content/uploads/longtermrecoveryguide-final2012.pdf
- National Disaster Recovery Framework Resources: https://www.fema.gov/emergency-managers/national-preparedness/frameworks/recovery
- National Mitigation Framework: https://www.fema.gov/emergency-managers/national-preparedness/frameworks/mitigation
- National Preparedness Goal: https://www.fema.gov/emergency-managers/national-preparedness/goal
- National Preparedness System: https://www.fema.gov/emergency-managers/national-preparedness/system
- National Prevention Framework: https://www.fema.gov/emergency-managers/national-preparedness/frameworks
- National Protection Framework: https://www.fema.gov/emergency-managers/national-preparedness/frameworks
- National Resilience Guidance: National Resilience Guidance | FEMA.gov
- National Response Framework: https://www.fema.gov/emergency-managers/national-preparedness/frameworks/response

- Natural & Cultural Resources RSF Overview: https://www.fema.gov/emergency-managers/national-preparedness/frameworks/recovery/recovery-support-functions/natural-cultural-resources-rsf
- Presidential Policy Directive-8: https://www.dhs.gov/xlibrary/assets/presidential-policy-directive-8-national-preparedness.pdf
- Small Business Administration Ascent Learning Journey Disaster and Economic Recovery: https://www.sba.gov/
- Small Business Administration Business Resilience Guide: https://www.sba.gov/document/support-business-resilience-guide
- Small Business Development Centers: https://www.sba.gov/local-assistance/resource-partners/small-business-development-centers-sbdc
- United Federal Environment and Historic Preservation Review Resources: https://www.fema.gov/emergency-managers/practitioners/environmental-historic/review
- U.S. Department of Education Natural Disaster Resources: https://www.ed.gov/disasterrelief
- U.S. Global Change Research Program, Fifth National Climate Assessment, 2023: https://nca2023.globalchange.gov/
- FEMA Planning Guidance: https://www.fema.gov/emergency-managers/national-preparedness/plan

STATE AND TERRITORY RESOURCE LINKS:

- FEMA Assistance for Governments and Private Non-Profits After a Disaster: https://www.fema.gov/assistance/public
- Pre-Disaster Recovery Guide for State Governments: https://www.fema.gov/sites/default/files/2020-06/pre-disaster_recovery_planning_guide_state_governments.pdf
- Request For Presidential Disaster Declaration: https://www.fema.gov/disaster/request-for-presidential-disaster-declaration

TRIBAL NATION RESOURCE LINKS:

- 2022-2026 FEMA National Tribal Strategy: https://www.fema.gov/sites/default/files/documents/fema_national-tribal-strategy_08182022.pdf
- FEMA Assistance for Tribal Governments: https://www.fema.gov/fact-sheet/fema-assistance-tribal-governments
- FEMA Assistance for Governments and Private Non-Profits After a Disaster: https://www.fema.gov/assistance/public
- FEMA Tribal Affairs Resources: https://www.fema.gov/about/organization/tribes
- FEMA Tribal Funding, Mitigation, and Planning Resources: https://www.fema.gov/about/organization/tribes/funding-mitigation-planning-resources#mitigation
- Pre-Disaster Recovery Guide for Tribal Governments: https://www.fema.gov/sites/default/files/2020-07/pre-disaster-recovery-planning-guide-for-tribal-government.pdf

- Request For Presidential Disaster Declaration: https://www.fema.gov/disaster/request-for-presidential-disaster-declaration
- Tribal Declarations Pilot Guidance: https://www.fema.gov/disaster/tribal-declarations
- U.S. Department of Health and Human Services American Indian & Alaskan Native Disaster Preparedness Resource: https://aspr.hhs.gov/behavioral-health/Pages/tribal-preparedness.aspx

LOCAL GOVERNMENT RESOURCE LINKS:

- Achieving Equitable Recovery: A Post-Disaster Guide for Local Officials and Leaders https://www.fema.gov/sites/default/files/documents/fema_equitable-recovery-post-disaster-guide-local-officials-leaders.pdf
- FEMA Assistance for Governments and Private Non-Profits After a Disaster: https://www.fema.gov/assistance/public
- Local Elected and Appointed Officials Guide: Roles and Resources in Emergency Management: https://www.fema.gov/sites/default/files/documents/fema_local-elected-officials-guide_2022.pdf
- Pre-Disaster Recovery Guide for Local Governments: https://www.fema.gov/sites/default/files/2020-06/pre-disaster_recovery_planning_guide_local_governments.pdf

> # Appendix F: National Preparedness Goal Core Capabilities

The table below outlines the Recovery Core Capabilities found in the National Preparedness Goal (NPG).

Table 5: NPG Recovery Core Capabilities

Core Capability	Description
Planning	Conduct a systematic process engaging the whole community as appropriate in the development of executable strategic, operational, and/or tactical-level approaches to meet defined objectives.
Public Information and Warning	Deliver coordinated, prompt, reliable, and actionable information to the whole community through the use of clear, consistent, accessible, and culturally and linguistically appropriate methods to effectively relay information regarding any threat or hazard and, as appropriate, the actions being taken, and the assistance being made available.
Operational Coordination	Establish and maintain a unified and coordinated operational structure and process that appropriately integrates all critical partners and supports the execution of core capabilities.
Economic Recovery	Return economic and business activities (including food and agriculture) to a healthy state and develop new business and employment opportunities that result in an economically viable community.
Health and Social Services	Restore and improve health and social services capabilities and networks to promote the resilience, independence, health (including behavioral health), and well-being of the whole community.
Housing	Implement housing solutions that effectively support the needs of the whole community and contribute to its sustainability and resilience.
Infrastructure Systems	Stabilize critical infrastructure functions, minimize health and safety threats, and efficiently restore and revitalize systems and services to support a viable, resilient community.
Natural and Cultural Resources	Protect natural and cultural resources and historic properties through appropriate planning, mitigation, response, and recovery actions to preserve, conserve, rehabilitate, and restore them consistent with post-disaster community priorities and best practices and in compliance with applicable environmental and historic preservation laws and executive orders.

Appendix G: Document Updates and Maintenance

This third edition of the NDRF reflects the insights and lessons learned from real-world incidents and the implementation of the National Preparedness System. It emphasizes conducting preparedness activities with resilience in mind - not just preparing for threats and hazards but also adapting to changing conditions and ensuring an ability to withstand and recover rapidly from adverse conditions and disruptions. Solutions will be based on the seven resilience principles from the National Resilience Guidance. Major updates within the Third Edition include:

- Streamlining wherever possible with an emphasis on plain language.
- Recognizing that recovery is not time-bound and must be community-driven and executed toward shared goals.
- Simplifying the RSF agency naming conventions from three tiers to two: coordinating agencies and participating agencies and organizations.
- Updating the names of two RSFs: Community Assistance RSF, formerly Community Planning and Capacity Building RSF, and Health, Education, and Human Services RSF, formerly Health and Social Services RSF.

The NDRF will be regularly reviewed to evaluate its consistency with existing and new policies, evolving conditions, and the experience gained from its use. The NDRF will be reviewed to accomplish the following:

- Assess and update information on the core capabilities in support of preparedness goals and objectives.
- Ensure that the NDRF adequately reflects the organization of responsible entities.
- Ensure that the NDRF is consistent with the other four mission areas.
- Update processes based on changes in the national threat/hazard environment.
- Incorporate lessons learned and effective practices from day-to-day operations, exercises, and actual disasters and alerts.
- Reflect progress in the Nation's recovery mission and the need to execute new laws, executive orders, and presidential directives, as well as strategic changes to national priorities and guidance, critical tasks, and/or national capabilities.

In reviewing the NDRF, the federal government will consider effective practices (i.e., continuity planning), lessons learned from exercises and operations, and pertinent new processes and technologies. Lastly, the NDRF is not intended as a detailed operational guide for recovery partners. It is a framework for how the nation mobilizes resources for disaster recovery. Specific operational doctrine and plans will be developed separately.